Crown Keepers

Sally Fear

Crown Keepers *of the* New Forest
Sally Fear

Most people all over the world seem to like keeping connections with their past. Ancient buildings and works of art are preserved and cared for. Landscapes do not fare so well when land is needed for homes, other buildings and for such necessities as roads. In that respect, the New Forest is almost unique. It has been spared encroachment and development in a country where the population has soared from a few million, only a couple of centuries ago, to something like 60 million today.

The New Forest has not only survived, it has thrived and that is due to the people who have given it tender loving care ever since it was set aside by King William over a thousand years ago. This book records their wonderfully successful work over that long period. It is the sympathetic understanding of the problems of managing such an area in order to preserve its character and 'lifestyle' that has made it possible for our generation, and future generations, to admire and enjoy this relic of our distant history. Hemmed in, as it is, by developing civilisation, it needs particularly sensitive management if it is to retain any semblance of a natural wilderness. Such management only comes from a deep and sympathetic understanding of the natural processes which govern the existence of the Forest.

I very much welcome this dramatic record of the work of the Keepers of the New Forest. Their evident success, in the face of dramatic changes elsewhere, displays a knowledgeable commitment, which is well beyond the comprehension of the casual visitor, and all the more skilful because it is not evident.

Introduction

Introduction
Robin Page

I haven't visited the New Forest properly for over 40 years, when I was researching a book of my own – *The Hunter and the Hunted*. The fact that I have not been back is simply the product of a busy life. I have been through it several times on my way to Hardy Country in Dorset on the A31 but always too fast because of too little time. It has been my loss, a loss emphasised by Sally Fear's outstanding book. It took me back to that great wild stretch of a land – a royal hunting forest of trees, heather and bog that goes back into history hundreds of years and can still give us a glimpse of almost wild Britain. A place where wildlife and the seasons can be felt, smelt and watched as they progress through the year. Still there is birdsong, the sound of rutting deer, the scent of blossom and the fragile wings of butterflies.

There are men working too, with occupations going back generations – they are the Crown Keepers of the New Forest who manage the wildlife of this enchanting place. They watch, listen, intervene, improve, sigh and smile. They really are the keepers of the New Forest with a proud pedigree.

Rural jobs and traditions still manage to hang on, just, in urban, overcrowded Britain. But suddenly a bureaucrat somewhere, desk-bound and surrounded by a tangle of red tape, decided that the time was up for the Crown Keepers – their title and their work had no place in modern 'countryside management'. This is when Sally Fear arrived on the scene with pen and camera.

I married a widow named Lulu. It can be tough – realignment and a change of direction. Sally became a widow and her change of direction took her to her new husband's house in the New Forest, and to this book. As a professional photographer she had travelled the world and contributed to many major newspapers and magazines. Suddenly her focus changed, it turned to the Commoners and then the Crown Keepers of the New Forest on her new doorstep.

What a book of feeling, beauty and understanding. A book capturing the people of the forest and the wildlife. Look at the book: smell autumn, listen to the spring, feel the heat of summer and hear the silence of winter. It is a book that took more than five years to produce. On occasions it took a week to capture the fleeting glimpse of a butterfly in the right light. The rutting red deer stag was so overcome with lust that she was ignored completely – and then there were the Keepers themselves ensuring healthy habitats and populations. Sally rejects the idea of a tinsel-coated countryside – she has produced a book dealing with the real countryside – and the end product is exceptional.

In addition it is a very brave book. Sally Fear has backed her own beliefs and principles and published the book herself. She has had the courage to follow her instincts to show people and wildlife in a landscape of beauty threatened by change all around it. What a book – it is a document that I will value; it is too good for a coffee table – it is going into my most important book case.

A roe doe with her young kid (there was a twin too but it disappeared into the undergrowth).

Spring

You can cut all the flowers but you cannot keep spring from coming.

Pablo Neruda

The New Forest countryside noticeably brightens in spring. The Keepers are finishing off the controlled burning in February and March. Hazel catkins decorate the edge of the woodland inclosures, the browns of winter twigs become clothed in palettes of vivid greens. The sound of birdsong conveys a feeling of optimism. There is buoyancy in the air. The curlew and lapwing have arrived in the wet valleys of the open heath; the woodlark sings a mellow song on the woodland edge; the cock Dartford warbler sings from the top of a gorse bush on a bright March day; the chiffchaff sings with its monotonous high pitched 'chiff-chaff' or 'zip-zap'. Early April you hear the distinctive call of the first cuckoo and you see your first brimstone butterfly (known locally as the February Pleasure). Violets adorn the sheltered ride edges and are an important food source for the early butterflies.

A concerted effort is made by all Keepers to target pairs of corvids (crows and magpies) that have set up territories to try and allow the more vulnerable species to nest successfully without predation. Signage is used to advise the public of the presence of ground nesting birds and to request them to keep their dogs under strict control.

The bluebell *Hyacinthoides non-scriptus* woods are another great joy. They cover the floors of the inclosures like a beautiful wash of colour. It is a good sight after the grey of winter woodland. Bluebells are quintessentially British and the New Forest has 34 square kilometres of broad-leaved inclosures

where bluebells flourish under the canopy of trees. The mix of brand new beech-leaf green and purple-blue is vibrant and catches the morning light throughout April and May. The woodlands are also home to wood anemones, early flowering orchids, wild garlic (ramsons), lesser celandines and primroses. The first damselflies and demoiselles are to be seen and the deer antlers start growing after the old ones are cast when testosterone levels have fallen in mid-March and April after the rut.

When a stag or buck's testosterone levels fall, it causes a weakening in the tissue and bone at the antler base (pedicle) to the point where the antlers simply fall off. This process can happen quickly; antlers that are firmly attached one day can weaken and fall off within 24 to 48 hours. A male in peak

Previous spread: Cuckooflower also known as Lady's Smock *Cardamine pratensis*.
Left: A new born fallow fawn.
Opposite top: Foxglove *Digitalis purpurea*.
Opposite bottom: Bluebells *Hyacinthoides non-scriptus* and Wood Spurge *Euphorbia amygdaloides*.

physical health will shed his antlers later than a weaker one, while injured deer often shed their antlers early. Shedding antlers causes them no discomfort. The female deer are looking shabby as their new summer coats start to grow and the old winter jackets fall out.

Red deer cast their antlers in February-March, sika in March-April, fallow in March-April, muntjac in May-June and roe not until November-December. Early spring is a good time to look for freshly cast antlers. The male of all British indigenous and introduced deer cast their antlers and grow a new set each year.

Cast antlers are bone and therefore a rich source of phosphorus and calcium, so old antlers are often heavily chewed by mice, squirrels and even deer themselves. Antlers can be cast one at a time or a pair can sometimes be found close together before they are gnawed. Deer chew antlers using molars in the side of their mouth (they only have incisors in the lower jaw). Mice, voles and squirrels gnaw antlers with their incisors.

The young red, sika, roe and fallow are born at this time of year in May and June and are hidden by their mothers among the bracken and long grass. Dog walkers are asked to keep their dogs on the lead. Newborns are born scentless and immobile; therefore hiding a fawn or calf for the first few weeks of their life is the best way a mother can protect them from predators.

New Forest Keepers

Clockwise from top left: Jonathan Cook actioning a break in the byelaws on his beat. Network Rail fencing was reported in poor condition due to fallen trees. They met with Graham Wilson estates Keeper and Patrick Cook beat Keeper. Keepers Ian Young and Maarten Ledeboer on squirrel control. Some years squirrels have to be controlled to protect trees and the birds' nests. Maarten and Ian drive commoners' stock out of the inclosure where they stray when gates are left open. This means less food for the deer. Ponies and cattle browse more intensively and destroy valuable ground cover.

The Keepers' main job is the care and management of the deer and all flora and fauna. However there are many other less enjoyable jobs that come under their remit. Unlike any other Forestry Commission staff, they work a 24-hour roster, they work in pairs as beat partners and provide Forest-wide cover seven days a week. They are key in counteracting more modern threats to this peaceful Forest; like the drug culture and the frequent drug fuelled rave parties on Crown Lands, the use of Forest car parks for illicit acts and sexual activity, wild camping, fires and arson, missing persons, suicide, 4x4 and motorbike trespass, antisocial behaviour and a myriad other issues directly linked with the exponential increase in public pressure on our Forest today.

The New Forest differs from other Forestry Commission districts in that only a small percentage of the 144 square miles that the Keepers cover is under commercial forestry. They act as guardians to numerous Forest towns, villages, hamlets and the expanse of open forest (outside of the inclosures) that consist of many important habitats for which the New Forest is famous.

Over this, the Keeper team act as 'watchdogs' within the Forestry Commission, ensuring that forestry practices are carried out in a sustainable way and do not damage species, habitats, etc.

Opposite: Squirrel control.

Deer *on the* New Forest

Deer are instantly recognisable, even if you have never seen a wild deer. The handsome antlers of a mature stag or buck are unique in the animal world. Pictures of deer are everywhere in the New Forest – on road signs, pub signs, postcards and calendars. They embrace a spirit of freedom of the wild.

They are beautiful creatures and an important part of our natural heritage and an integral part of the landscape. The New Forest has always been renowned for its deer, particularly when royalty used it as a hunting ground. There are only two truly native species of deer within Britain: the roe deer *Capreolus capreolus* and red deer *Cervus elaphus*. The other three species found within the New Forest are fallow deer *Dama dama* – which are the most common – sika *Cervus nippon* and muntjac *Muntiacus reevesii*. These have all been introduced, released or escaped into the environment.

It is recognised that too many deer can have a damaging effect on certain sensitive habitats and can restrict tree establishment. Ensuring that deer stay healthy, have appropriate habitats and are well managed is key to a sustainable future. They are herbivores and browse a wide variety of plants from grasses and heather to shrubs and trees. They do not have a top set of front incisors but instead have a hard pad that acts to tear vegetation rather than cut it. They are active throughout the day and night but are most likely to be active at dawn and dusk.

When numbers of deer become too great for their habitat to support them, they can have a detrimental impact on plant species diversity and can cause damage to agriculture and forestry. Today, under the supervision of Head Keeper Andy Page, the New Forest Keepers are managing deer populations sensitively and humanely. They work closely with neighbouring landowners and partners including the British Deer Society and the Deer Initiative.

It is usually quite difficult for the public to see deer. However, red and fallow can often be viewed from the fence line of Queens Meadow. People and dogs are forbidden to go into Queens Meadow so the deer feel safe to browse in the open. In addition, Keeper Andy Shore feeds a herd of fallow deer

Above: Fallow buck in Autumn.
Opposite: Red stag in velvet.

Spring

regularly in the summer at Bolderwood, where there is a purpose-built viewing platform. There is also a private herd of red deer at Burley Park and a regular tractor and trailer safari for visitors.

The red deer *Cervus elaphus* is Britain's largest land wild mammal and is a true native species. Red deer migrated to Britain from Europe at the end of the ice age. They were hunted extensively by Mesolithic man as a source of food, skins and tools made from bones and antlers. They are kept at a level of around 80 head in the Crown lands of the New Forest. They are rich red-brown in colour with a pale brown patch on the rump. They are herding animals that utilise the woodland and surrounding heathland for feeding. The Forestry Commission aims to maintain the herds in the west of the Forest, to avoid the risk of cross-breeding with sika.

Stags tend to move off the Forest onto outlying farmland and private estates after the rut has finished, at the end of October. The hinds usually remain in their highest concentrations around the central parts of the New Forest. Red deer are red-coloured in summer. This changes to greyish-brown in winter to match the vegetation. Calves are born with a spotted pelage which fades with maturity. The stags' antlers are the species' most distinguishing feature. They are highly branched and the branches increase with age, with multiple points on each antler. The angle of the forward point from the main antler beam is about 90° (unlike the sika). Antlers are cast during March-April and begin to regrow to be fully formed and clear of velvet in August-September. The mating season, known as the rut, begins in mid-September and continues to late October. Hinds normally give birth to single calves from late May to June.

Roe deer *Capreolus capreolus* are native to Britain, having been present since the Ice Age. They are territorial and secretive, generally keeping to dense undergrowth.

Numbers of roe are very difficult to gauge but it is thought that there are around 350 to 400 on the Crown lands of the New Forest. They are essentially woodland animals, and can be seen in any of the more wooded areas of the New Forest at any time of year. Early morning or evening are the best times to see them, feeding in small groups at the edges of the woodlands or in nearby fields.

They are small – about the size of a small sheep or goat. They are bright red-brown in summer and greyer in winter, with a characteristic pale rump that is easily seen as they run away from you. Roe deer are dainty creatures. They are different from the other deer in that the bucks grow their antlers in winter.

During the breeding season, does attract bucks with a high-pitched piping call. Bucks respond with a rasping noise during courtship. The roe deer kids make a high-pitched whistle to attract their mothers when they become lost. Bucks defend a territory from the start of spring in April until the end of August. The roe deer rut occurs between late July

and early August, much earlier than other species of deer. During this time bucks will pursue does and chase other bucks entering their territories. However, the kids are born at the same time of year as other deer species due to delayed implantation, a process in which the fertilised embryo does not attach to the womb until a few months later. Roe deer are the only hoofed animal to do this. Does give birth between mid-May and mid-June, usually to twins or a single kid. The young suckle within a few hours of birth. They are regularly left alone, lying still among vegetation. Their coat, dappled for about the first six weeks, helps to camouflage them. If there are twins they are left separately.

Until recently it was thought that the Normans introduced fallow deer *Dama dama* to Great Britain for hunting in the royal forests. However, recent finds at Fishbourne Roman Palace show that fallow deer were introduced into southern England in the 1st century AD. It is not known whether these escaped to form a feral colony, or whether they died out and were reintroduced by the Normans. They have the longest continuous lineage of any deer species on the Forest.

The New Forest was William the Conqueror's first hunting forest in England, and the hunting of fallow bucks took place for over 900 years until the Buckhounds voluntarily disbanded in 1997. In the 17th century the deer census in the New Forest reported that the population of fallow deer stood at 7,500. After the 1851 Deer Removal Act they were the only species that managed to escape the cull and the 1900 population was around 200. From then on numbers have increased.

Today fallow deer are managed at 1,000 in the New Forest, and are the most commonly seen deer. In the summer months most fallow deer have a light chestnut coat with white spots; this then changes to an unspotted grey-brown coat in the winter months. There is also the Menil variety, a paler colour with white spot; Melanistic, which is almost entirely black or chocolate; and white to pale sandy, turning increasingly white with age. White fallow deer were once known as 'Judas' deer because their colour gave away the presence of the herd to poachers. Mature males are the only species in Britain with palmate antlers. Does and their young give short barks when alarmed. Bucks groan loudly during the breeding season in October-November and may form stands, which are areas where small territories are defended against their competitors.

They range over large areas but they can cause a great deal of damage by feeding on buds and leaves, and they will also strip bark from trees. Usually the doe gives birth to a single fawn between late May and mid-June. Both sexes live in single-sex groups for most of the year, only getting together at the time of the rut.

Sika *Cervus nippon* are originally from Japan. The New Forest sika are descendants of those given to the 2nd Baron Montagu at Beaulieu by King Edward VII in 1904. Shortly after, two sika deer

escaped to set up home in the wild. In 1905 two more were deliberately released, giving birth to the growing population of today's New Forest herd. The New Forest herd is considered to be of a clean bloodline, with no intermixing of other subspecies, or hybridization with red deer. The Forestry Commission keeps the sika in the Beaulieu area to avoid cross-breeding with the red deer that are found in the west of the New Forest. Sika numbers are maintained at about 70.

Sika are sensitive to human disturbance and hide in woodland by day, venturing out at night. They tend to be solitary for most of the year and only form small groups in winter. During the rut in October and November, you are more likely to hear the eerie scream of the stags than to see them. The deer live in single-sex groups for most of the year, only coming together during the breeding season and in winter when times are harder. They give birth from early May to July and they usually have a single calf. They mate from late September to November. Like fallow deer, sika stags defend a small rutting territory from competitors but may also defend a harem of hinds if gathered together, like the red deer. The courting and mating of the sika is dependent on the terrain and habitat of the individuals.

Sika are a medium- to large-sized deer and are similar to fallow deer in coat colour. The stag's antlers are widely spaced and the angle of the forward point from the main antler beam is about 45°. They generally have a maximum of eight points

on their antlers, except in the New Forest where sika stags can produce more. A fine example can be seen in the Verderers' Court in Lyndhurst.

Reeves' muntjac *Muntiacus reevesi* are small, dog-sized creatures with long back legs. They are hump-backed and a bit bigger than a fox. Ginger in colour, they are often called barking deer as they repeatedly bark loudly; they also scream or squeak when alarmed. Muntjac are not often seen in the New Forest, but numbers are increasing, so the Forestry Commission has a policy of culling them because they represent a threat to the ground flora.

Muntjac were named in 1812 after John Reeves of the East India Company. The deer originated in Southeast Asia and were introduced to Britain by the Duke of Bedford at Woburn Park in the early 20th century. Feral populations were quick to establish from both escapees and deliberate releases. Now they are widespread in southern and central England. Muntjac like cover and live predominantly in woods with plenty of scrub in the understorey. The bucks have short, slightly hooked antlers born on long pedicels, sloping strongly backwards, and long protruding canines; the does have single kids. They are capable of breeding at seven months old and can breed all year round, with a doe able to conceive again within days of giving birth. She can be almost continuously pregnant and can produce three kids in two years. They are generally solitary or found in pairs: a doe with a kid or a buck with a doe.

Ringing Goshawk Chicks

Clockwise from top left: Keepers Matthew Davies (left) and Andy Page look up at the goshawk nest. Andy Page makes the uncomfortable 28m climb up to the nest. Down on the ground Andy Page measures the chick's wing span. He then weighs the chick by carefully placing it in a soft bag and hangs it on scales. Goshawk chick aged approximately 3-4 weeks after being ringed. Goshawk chicks aged approximately 2-3 weeks waiting to be weighed, measured and ringed.

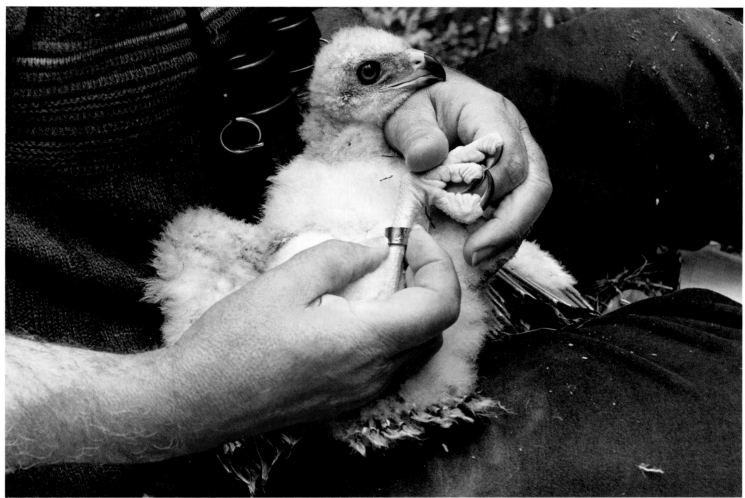

'The phantoms of the forest', as goshawks are sometimes known, live and nest in large mature woods and forests but also hunt in the open countryside. Only 500 breeding pairs exist in the UK, including around 20 pairs resident to the New Forest.

All New Forest goshawk nests are monitored to record their productivity, which reflects the health of the population and therefore the health and diversity of the managed woodlands in which they live.

Their nests are usually in a Douglas fir at a height of 28 metres. Keepers Andy Page and Matt Davies scale the trees to the nest and gently place the chicks in a small padded bag that they lower to the ground. An experienced and licensed ringer fits a unique ring to the leg of each chick, which can be used to identify individual birds in the future. The sex of the chicks is identified by weight, wing and leg measurements as at this stage the females are significantly heavier and also have a longer leg than the males. There is always the hope that one of the adults will be one that they ringed in previous years.

Top: Goshawk chick aged approximately 3 weeks. Middle: Andy Page checks that the goshawk chick's new ring is comfortable.

Spring

The New Forest is an area of international importance. It is Britain's richest 'nature reserve'.

Colin Tubbs

Previous spread: Red deer in spring when they have a motley appearance while losing their winter coat. The moulted pins (hair) is ideal nesting material for birds.
Opposite: Sika hinds browsing the fresh spring growth.
Above: The browse line is the comfortable height that deer can reach.

Hunting *with the* Minkhounds

The Mink Hunt was formed in 1978 and covers Hampshire, Wiltshire and Dorset. Known as the Ytene, they hunted the country formally hunted by the Courtenay Tracy Otterhounds. It is interesting to note that Otterhound packs all over the country identified a problem with the otter population and imposed a voluntary ban on hunting them.

The country hunted extends to the rivers and their tributaries between Portsmouth and Weymouth and northwards to include the Bristol Avon. The Minkhounds have been very effective in ridding the waterways of the North American predator. As well as depleting the population of water voles (Ratty from *Wind in the Willows*), the non-native carnivorous mink also decimate the eggs and young of native waterfowl, ground nesting birds, and particularly Kingfishers. Mink are more of a threat than foxes because they hunt all day, whereas foxes normally hunt at first and last light.

Alas! In 2004 the Hunting Act banned mink hunting and now rats are searched for.

At the request of a bequeathment, the Hunt has changed its name back to The Courtenay Tracy.

Despite the hunting of mink being outlawed there are still 20 registered minkhound packs in England and Wales. The fox is certainly not the quarry, and neither until repeal is the mink, but to those who follow the minkhounds, the experience they offer is incomparable. Before the ban was imposed the best mink hunting took place on dry days: a relatively low

Top: Joint Master Tony Smart.
Middle: Tony Smart with hounds and followers.

Clockwise from top left: Tony Smart leads the hounds out of the water. Searching the tree roots for rats. A hound gets left behind. Minkhounds. Tony Smart watches the hounds searching for rats in the tree roots. Overleaf: Tony Smart leads the Courtenay Tracy Minkhounds pack at the edge of the water.

river meant that the hounds could pick up a scent on the exposed muddy banks. It was always difficult early on in the season as the mink bitches would be in kit, this means that in order to protect themselves from predators they do not lay a scent.

The hunting ban has not had a noticeable impact on the eagerness and enthusiasm for mink hunting. The followers are as loyal as ever and there are just as many hounds as before the ban. Minkhounds are a mix of English and Welsh foxhounds, but many are descendants of the original otterhounds.

Grey Squirrel *and* Magpie Management

Andy Shore out on corbid (crows and magpies) control. Corbids predate the birds' nests. He would also be on the look out for mink on the river bank.

Top and middle: Ian Young sets a trap for squirrels in woodland where there has been considerable damage to trees and birds' nests. Squirrels caught in traps. Ian Young moving the traps to another location. The squirrels he caught have been humanely despatched. Transferring a trapped squirrel into a sack for humane despatch.

Bottom: The targeted magpies have been successfully caught in the Larsen trap. Removing the magpies from the Larsen trap. A Larsen trap is good because if you catch something that you do not want you can let it go.

Electric
Fish Survey

Dominic Longley with
Rebecca Long conducting
the fish survey on Graham
Wilson's beat. They
briefly stun the fish with
a mild electric shock and
catch it in a landing net
for identification and
measuring.

'We conducted three fish population surveys in July 2013, using a battery-powered backpack electric fishing unit. All three surveys were for the long-term monitoring of the New Forest's wild brown trout *Salmo trutta*, many of which become sea trout, feeding and growing at sea before returning to these streams to spawn in winter.

'At these three sites we caught, in total: 21 brown trout (mostly juveniles), 22 minnows, 23 stone loach, 14 brook lamprey, 39 bullhead and four eel.

'These catches are relatively low. In a summer where flow in the streams remains consistently high, we would expect to catch all these species in far greater numbers.'

Dominic Longley Environment Agency fish scientist

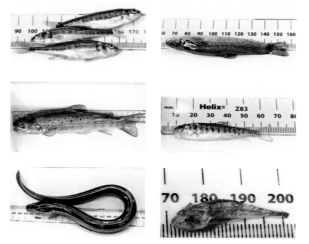

Clockwise from top left:
Minnows, stone loach, one-year-old brown trout *Salmo trutta*, bullhead, European eel, two- or three-year-old brown trout *Salmo trutta*

Public
Management

As Guardians of the the New Forest, the Keepers have to protect the Forest against thoughtless actions:

Clockwise from top left: A member of the public shares Keeper Tim Creed's disgust at fly-tipping in a car park. Incidents of waste being dumped in the New Forest have increased by almost 30% over the last year. Each time rubbish is fly-tipped on the Forest a Keeper has to deal with it. The Forestry Commission sets aside £70,000 a year to deal with litter and waste removal that could be better spent on things like replanting trees.

Some young people have unlawfully built a den on the Forest cutting Forest wood and generally damaging Crown property. Keeper Alan Stride explains why they cannot do this.

Keeper Graham Wilson talks to a camper about why he is not allowed to pitch his tent where he wishes – even though his feet were tired from walking.

Commoner Ernie Mansbridge called his friend Keeper Graham Wilson when he discovered that vandals had stolen a Forest gate. This left the ponies and cattle vulnerable as they could wander out on to the roads. Graham put a temporary gate in place until a new one was found.

Firearms Skills Test

'It seemed very strange at first, training my old colleagues; remember that some of them I had worked with on a daily basis for 25 years. They did not cut me any slack and so I too gave no quarter when it came to the skills test (remember the collective noun for a group of NF keepers is a mischief!).

'But on the whole it is a very serious subject for the Forestry Commission and the Keepers; I had their full attention and cooperation during the course.

'The range test day is a culmination of a week-long, full bore firearm course, covering various shooting aspects of the deer management part of the very diverse role of a New Forest Keeper.

'The course covers:

Firearms users' responsibilities

Firearm handling, Safety and Maintenance

Health and Safety requirements

Zeroing and shooting principles

'The keepers were instructed, coached and practised shooting safely from a number of different firing positions.

'The Shooting skills test:

Prone 100m

Shooting from high seat 100m

Sitting shooting with or without sticks 75m

Standing shooting with or without sticks 40m

Shooting from vehicle 100m

Close range humane dispatch with rifle 5m

'The test has to be passed as Keepers must be licensed to carry a Forestry Commission firearm

Above: The deer silhouettes were the targets that the Keepers were tested on. Opposite top: Robert Colin-Stokes about to test one of the Keepers. Opposite bottom: Tim Creed being examined by Robert Colin-Stokes. Overleaf: Keepers have a keen interest in how their colleagues are doing.

Clockwise from top left:
Howard Taylor prepares to
take a shot from his vehicle.
Graham Wilson watches
through a spotting scope.
Keepers go down nearer
the target to inspect how
well they did. Tim Creed
is examined from the
shooting position stand.

and use the firearm on the public forest estate.
The skills test then has to be passed yearly: it is
usually conducted by the Head Keeper until the
next update of the firearms course comes around
again when I fully skills test them again.

'The industry standard is all shots in a 4in circle,
the Keepers all shoot a much tighter group than that
(1-2 in groups).

'The delegates all feel very much happier once
they have completed the test and then the Keepers'
peer pressure and the joking nature of the New
Forest Keepers really comes out!'

Robert Colin-Stokes (former Keeper),
Technical Trainer Wildlife & Environment
Learning & Development Forestry Commission

Keeper Beats
and Cottages

Anderwood Cottage. Howard Taylor with his wife Anna and their daughters Daisy (left) and Lauryn.

The Forestry Commission has no special way of dividing up the beats. It is usually a response to staffing levels and workloads at the time. They are mostly based around what has traditionally evolved as a Keeper's beat house or cottage. However this is not set in stone as houses can be given key status due to operational needs.

Most of the current Keepers' cottages were originally woodmen's cottages and not built for the Keepers at all. As the inclosures grew up and required less time and as the old Groom Keepers were replaced by Under Keepers, who as Gerald Lascelles states were just promoted labourers, they were placed in the old woodmen's cottages. Indeed some were Keeper/woodman. The detail is somewhat unclear.

Today's Keepers each have a beat partner so they can cover for each other and work together if they choose. Keepers' families are the integral foundation of their job and therefore also the protection of the Forest.

Clockwise from top left: Church Place Cottage. Patrick Cook, who is also a Commoner, lives here with his family. Longbeech Cottage. Tim Creed with his dog Fran lived here until he retired to France in 2015. Holidays Hill Cottage. Andy Shore with his wife Sandy Shore and their children Jim and Faith. Sandy is also a Keeper now and took over Tim Creed's beat in 2015. Kings Hat Cottage. Graham Wilson with his grandson George and George's uncle Sam. George's father Ben was away. Parkgrounds Cottage. Alan Stride and his family live here. Setthorns Cottage. Maarten Ledeboer with his wife Agnieszka, daughter Amelia and dog Hector.

Clockwise from top left:
Stockley Cottage. The
home of Jonathan Cook
and his family. Aldridge
Hill Cottage. The home of
retired Keeper Ian Young.
Linford Cottage. The home
of Head Keeper Andy Page.
Godhills Cottage. The home
of Matthew Davies, his wife
the Reverend Nicky Davies
and their two daughters.
Matt and Nicky Davies.

Forest life gets into your soul. That connection
between God's creation, creatures and people is
what has sustained me and led to my ordination as a
priest in the Church of England. Jesus says we must
be 'salt and light' to those we meet and there are many
folk who I would describe as the 'salt of the earth.'

The seasons dictate what happens. Every creature
and we belong. We are connected in an integral ecology
and a radical relatedness. I see God at the centre.

This book highlights Forest characters that work
unceasingly to manage and protect the life of the
Forest. My prayer is that future generations will be
able to meet with God in The New Forest and
experience the wonder of this beautiful place.
The Reverend Nicky Davies

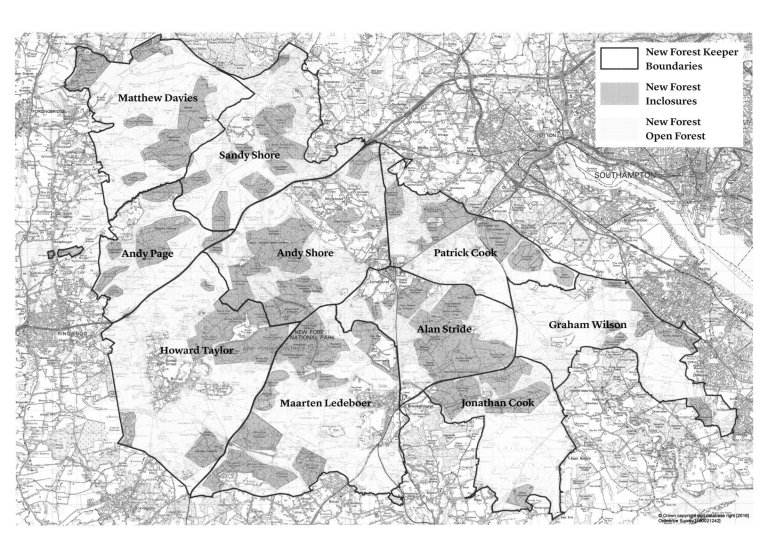

New Forest Keeper
Boundaries

New Forest
Inclosures

New Forest
Open Forest

Matthew Davies

Sandy Shore

Andy Page

Andy Shore

Patrick Cook

Alan Stride

Graham Wilson

Howard Taylor

Maarten Ledeboer

Jonathan Cook

FORDINGBRIDGE

SOUTHAMPTON

RINGWOOD

NEW FOREST
NATIONAL PARK

© Crown copyright and database right [2016]
Ordnance Survey [100021242]

Summer

Bees do have a smell, for their feet are dusted with spices from a million flowers.

Ray Bradbury

In early summer, heathland is bright with yellow gorse and bracken, while in wet, boggy places the rare early marsh orchid grows. Later in the summer, bell heather, cross-leaved heath and dwarf gorse come into flower, along with the dodder and harebells. It's a good time for orchids too – the common-spotted, heath-spotted and lesser butterfly orchids are in flower on the heathlands, while in the valley mires the rare, tiny bog orchid is starting to bloom.

The bright flowers of yellow irises appear in the wetland fringes. In and around the wetter areas of the New Forest, fluffy white common cottongrass (also called multi-headed bog cotton) grows. They are at their most conspicuous in early summer. They ripple in the breeze and contrast with surrounding expanses of green and straw-coloured vegetation. The plant is unmistakable when in flower, grows to a height of around 60cm and has relatively long-stalked clusters of nodding flowers. Nowadays cottongrass simply has scenic value and serves to warn the unwary of wet places ahead, but not so long ago they were used for stuffing pillows and mattresses, for making candlewicks and, along with sphagnum moss, for First World War wound dressings.

Beautiful wild flowers are springing up everywhere. The bracken is cloaking vast areas of heathland. At this time of year it makes a vital contribution to the Forest's ecology. It provides cover for the wild

gladiolus now starting to flower and only found in the New Forest. Only a small proportion of the plants bloom in any one year, which makes finding them all the more exciting – they are so well hidden under the fern fronds.

The bracken also makes excellent shelter for the newborn fawn that will be left within it for hours at a time while the doe feeds up after giving birth. All the species of deer hide their newborn young. They may seem abandoned but each mother knows just where she has left her offspring. They are a sight to enjoy but should be left undisturbed. The adult deer all have their summer coats and the antlers are growing on the male red, sika and fallow deer. The roe bucks' antlers start growing in November-December.

Newly emerged butterflies are on the wing and migrating birds such as swallows and swifts have returned. The Dartford warbler is likely to be on her second clutch of eggs. The hobby hawk is probably quartering (a slow, low hunting flight) the heaths in its search for flying insects.

At the end of July the roe deer are rutting.

The Forest is also crowded with tourists and campers that the Keepers have to manage alongside their other duties, particularly the campers who abandon the designated campsites and set up wild camps in remote parts of the Forest.

Wildflowers

The New Forest is well known for its rare and special plants that are able to thrive because of the traditional management of the Forest and the grazing of the Commoners' stock: the ponies, cattle and donkeys. The gravels, sands and clays which underlie the heaths, woods, bogs and lawns provide a range of habitats each suited to specialised flowers. Although the sands and gravels are mostly acidic and suit the drifts of purple heather and golden, coconut scented gorse, where they become wetter or covered with bracken may be found the spectacular wild gladiolus *Gladiolus illyricus*, found only in the New Forest, many different orchids, the pure blue lungwort *Pulmonaria longifolia*, marsh gentians *Gentianella palustris*, Bluebells *Hyacinthus non-scripta*, wood anemones *Anemone nemerosa*, and, in the north of the Forest,

Lily-of-the-Valley *Convallaria majalis*, is also found in scrubby patches of grassy heath.

In the bogs are the insectivorous plants, the sundews *Drosera spp.*, butterworts *Pinguicula spp.*, and bladderworts *Utricularia spp.* A patch of red sundew, glistening in the sun, may be seen with bright blue damselflies caught in the drops of insect catching 'glue' that covers its round or oblong crimson leaves, while the yellow flowers on delicate stems of the bladderwort are the only visible signs of a plant which traps tiny water fleas in underwater bladders. Among these may be found, with great difficulty, the little green bog orchid *Hammarbya paludosa* – a spike a few inches high with dozens of minute blooms.

Many of the plants are smaller than elsewhere as they have no need to grow tall to compete with

Top: Dog rose *Rosa canina*.
Middle: Harebell *Campanula rotundifolia*.

the hard-grazed vegetation surrounding them. This
can give the flowers a jewel-like quality which bears
closer inspection. The ability of the grazing stock to
selectively crop the palatable grasses and herbs which
grow around these tiny plants is amazing.
Alison Bolton New Forest Botanist

Clockwise from top left:
Heath spotted orchid
Dactylhoriza maculata.
Bramble *Rubus spp.* Yellow
iris *Iris pseudoacorus.* Oblong
leaved sundew *Drosera
intermedia.* Bee orchid
Ophrys apifera. Cotton grass
Eriophorum angustifolium.
Opposite: Lesser butterfly
orchid *Platanthera bifolia.*

Clockwise from top left: A red deer hind moves through Queens Meadow with her calf confident that she is safe from the public and their dogs. It is an area that has been set aside by the Forestry Commission for deer to browse in peace. The public are prohibited from entering and are requested to keep their dog on a lead in the surrounding areas. A red hind with her calf just outside Queens Meadow. A red stag in the woods. Red stags sunning themselves in the bracken, which also helps to keep away the flies.

Opposite top: Red deer calf in the long grass of Queens Meadow. Opposite bottom: Red deer hinds with their calves. Overleaf: Sika calf beside its lactating mother.

Sit Still, Look Long and Hold Yourself Quiet.

Arthur Cadman Deputy Surveyor 1959-1968

Sika calf full of the joys of summer.

Top: Muntjac doe.
Middle: Muntjac buck.
Bottom: Muntjac buck
eating a crab apple.
Overleaf: A herd of sika
stags in summer with
antlers in velvet.

Summer

Roe Deer Rut

As mentioned before, the roe rut is at a different time of year: the last week in July overflowing into first week of August. I have never photographed it because I am always exhibiting at the New Forest Show. However in 2015 I was there. Bucks were briskly moving in and out of the woods and then suddenly on both sides of my path there was a buck chasing a doe. I didn't know which way to turn.

Opposite: Roe buck heading towards a doe.
Above: Roe doe asleep in the woods.
Overleaf: A roe buck chases a doe through the woods, and was hopefully successful.

Below: A playful roe doe.
Opposite top: A roe doe
daintily makes her way
through the sunlit
woodland.
Opposite bottom: A roe
doe proudly stands with her
twin kids early morning.

Opposite top: A fallow doe
is pleased to find her fawn.
Opposite bottom: Fallow
doe, eating something
tasty, with fawn.
Below: Fallow bucks
at sunset.

Butterflies

Clockwise from top left: White Admiral *Ladoga Camila*. Clouded yellow *Colias Croceus* about to land. Pearl-bordered fritillary underwing *Boloria euphrosyne*. Pearl-bordered fritillary *Boloria euphrosyne* basking in a classic habitat. Opposite: Pearl-bordered fritillary *Boloria euphrosyne* in flight.

The butterfly fauna of the New Forest is as diverse as the range of habitats that exist there. The New Forest is the southern stronghold of the UK Biodiversity Action Plan high-priority species, such as the pearl-bordered fritillary *Boloria euphrosyne*, while some of the more widespread species that occur in the woodland inclosures can be in such abundance that the highest counts across Hampshire are frequently recorded there.

What makes these areas so precious? The diversity of the habitats are influenced by the soil types and vegetation cover, which through the skill of the Crown Keepers are managed to benefit the invertebrate fauna. The endangered pearl-bordered fritillary has an exacting habitat requirement for its larval development: the critical 'habitat patch' will be a gentle south-facing slope with a close juxtaposition of a basking substrate with its food plant, violets. The first fritillary of the spring, it has suffered yet again from prolonged mild, wet winter conditions. This is an issue the Keeper has no control over.

The dainty silver-studded blue *Plebeius argus* breeds mostly on the young shoots of the cross-leaved heath *Erica tetralix*, which is a plant more inclined to damp heathlands. Bell heather *Erica cinerea* and ling *Calluna vulgaris* may also be used. In the best of the woodlands, from Wootton in the southwest to Brockishill in the northeast, the ride-side vegetation can boast literally hundreds of summer butterflies flitting among a mosaic of knee-high grasses, and feasting on succulent spikes of nodding purple and clusters of frothy cream inflorescence.

Is this a solely natural habitat? Leave it to itself, and in most instances it would rapidly convert to rampant neglect. Woodland ride edges require periodic management in order to sustain the correct structure. The Keeper has an intimate understanding of his beat and will bring into play the appropriate management tools to address the issue, taking into account wildlife concerns as well as public access and enjoyment.

Butterflies of the heath include those also found in woodland, such as gatekeeper and large skipper, along with small heath, small copper and, where holly flourishes, the holly blue. The distinctive butter-yellow male brimstone can be observed where its food plant, alder buckthorn, exists close

by. In addition to the silver-studded blue, another priority heathland specialist is the beautifully mottled grayling, of high and late summer. The grayling lays its eggs on isolated tufts of sheep's fescue and good breeding potential exists on areas where burnt gorse affords protection. Long-standing gorse towards Broomy Bottom was burnt in early 2016 to assist the Forest's most prolific population of grayling, which occurs where Ocknell Plain slopes west on an area burnt in 2009, but where numbers have declined from 90 to 40.

The open woodlands, especially those with mature oaks and an understorey of bramble and violets, will support two of the larger and more stunning butterflies, the silver-washed fritillary and the white admiral. The elusive white admiral, unrivalled for its graceful and agile flight, spends much of its time in the canopy of towering oak trees lapping up aphid honeydew. The ancient and ornamental woods adjacent to the Highland Water, such as Brinken, offer an exceptional experience.

Woodlands with wide open rides and a diverse vegetation cover of grasses and flowering plants will support golden skippers, whites including brimstone, and fritillaries including dark-green. The marbled white is a delight in inclosures such as Wootton, and is conspicuous amid all the woodland browns in a spectacle of eye-catching and bewildering abundance.

John Ruppersbery New Forest Lepidopterist

Clockwise from top left: John Ruppersbery, New Forest Lepidopterist, talking with Keeper Jonathan Cook on his beat. Six-spot Burnet moth *Zygaena filipendulae* feeding on tufted vetch *vicia cracca*. Brimstone *Gonepteryx rhamni* sharing its thistle with a bee. Speckled wood *Pararge aegeria* feeding on heather *calluna vulgaris*. Silver-washed fritillary *Argynnis paphia* mating on beech leaves.

Clockwise from top left: Gatekeeper (also known as hedge brown) *Pyronia tithonus* sunning on a dead leaf. Ringlet *Aphantopus hyperantus*. Large skipper *Ochlodes sylvanus*. Female silver studded blue *Plebejus argus* feeding on crossed leaved heather *erica tetralix*. Small tortoiseshell underwing *Aglais urticae*. A quad of marbled white *Melanargia galathea* feeding on Black knapweed *centaurea nigra*. Small tortoiseshell *Aglais urticae* feeding on water mint flowers *mentha aquatica*. Silver-washed fritillary *Argynnis paphia* feeding on bramble flower *rubus fruticosus*. Male silver studded blue *Plebejus argus*. Silver-washed fritillary *Argynnis paphia* resting on bramble with a damaged wing (probably eaten by a bird).

Birds *of the* New Forest

With its unique mix of ancient oak and beech woods, mixed conifer Inclosures, heaths, mires, streams and ponds, the New Forest has always been a special place for birds.

Heavy grazing by ponies and cattle through traditional commoning practices, which have changed little over the years give a stability to the habitat that is hard to find replicated in the England of today. However as with much of our wildlife, a number of bird species are in slow decline due to man's increasing demands on the natural world. Where these declines are stark there are often compounding effects. Direct loss of habitat, persecution, pollution, disturbance and climate change all play a part.

In the last 30 years we have all but lost as breeding species from the New Forest, birds such as yellowhammer, whinchat, wheatear and lesser redpoll.

Populations of wood warbler, willow warbler, tree pipit, curlew and lapwing have fallen dramatically in the New Forest of recent years as are meadow pipit, linnet and many others currently.

Key New Forest species such as woodlark, Dartford warbler, hawfinch, firecrest and nightjar seem to be faring well and their populations remain healthy. The scarce and elusive honey buzzard and easily overlooked lesser-spotted woodpecker can still be found breeding while great grey shrike, hen harrier, redwing, fieldfare and merlin are wintering

A buzzard *Buteo buteo* chick that is probably on its first venture out of the nest.

species driven south from their more northern European haunts by snow and ice, and which tempt the bird watcher to the Forest when little other life seems present.

On the plus side we have seen the arrival of goshawk, peregrine falcon and raven as breeding species, but even here, the complexities of the predator prey relationship mean the arrival of goshawk has led to declines in sparrowhawk and hobby numbers while raven predate on ever dwindling nests of waders and others.

Key to much of the New Forest's attraction for bird life is the management of the habitat by the New Forest keepers and others through the annual burning programme, and our woodland

management and habitat restoration projects. Stacked against this are ever increasing demands for recreational use from a fast rising population who are already posing significant challenges for the Forest's birds and its wildlife.

Andy Page Head Keeper and Head of Wildlife

Autumn

Autumn

Autumn is a second spring when every leaf is a flower.
Albert Camus

S hafts of morning sunlight cut through the canopy of trees.

The 'roar' of the red stags that have returned from outside the Forest for the rut can be heard. In different parts of the Forest fallow bucks are 'groaning', and the sika stags are 'whistling'. The deer rut is one of Britain's great natural spectacles and sounds of it can be heard from mid to late September and last until the end of October. As with all natural spectacles, it's at its best at dawn and dusk and the public and photographers are strongly encouraged to stay well away. The Keepers, assisted by the Rangers and volunteers, are very busy protecting the deer and their privacy.

The leaves are falling and damp underfoot and there is also much to interest on the woodland floor. The New Forest is a thriving habitat for all wildlife and nature, especially fungi at this time of year. There are around 12,000 species of British fungi, with 2,700 of those found within the New Forest, coming in an often bewildering variety of shapes and sizes. They are a vital part of the forest ecosystem and are at their best in September, October and early November. Most fungi in the New Forest are not suitable for consumption, and some of them are poisonous, even deadly. New Forest fungi are under threat due to over-collecting. Picking is prohibited except for a personal 1.5 kilos. Commercial collecting is not permitted anywhere within the New Forest. The forest ecosystem has over 1,000 species of insects and creatures dependant on the fungi for

food. The Keepers are very busy policing the fungi pickers who get quite angry when caught and the Keepers have to destroy their harvest. So it is not an enjoyable job for either of them.

Tucked away between heath and mire in early autumn, there is always the possible treat of finding the bright blue trumpet-shaped flowers of the marsh gentian. Marsh gentians are incredibly rare plants that have significantly declined in recent years as a result of wetland drainage, climate change and irresponsible collecting. Quite a few survive in the New Forest where regular grazing by Commoners'

Opposite: Red stag in Autumn.
Above: Sweet chestnut which is food for deer.

stock and deer helps to reduce competition from more vigorous plants that would otherwise crowd out marsh gentians. Rotational, controlled burning has the same effect, and also produces areas of bare ground where marsh gentian seeds can better germinate.

How much of all this, I wonder, do the many cyclists speeding through the inclosure in their tight bright Lycra see and enjoy?

You cannot value what you do not know.
David Attenborough

When the rut is over the deer cull begins. All the Keepers have carefully done a deer count through the year and they start to cull the deer on their beat down to a healthy population.

The New Forest Hounds and the New Forest Beagles both have their opening Meets which are usually at the Royal Oak Fritham. Both are well attended and supported by local people, adults and children alike, asw well as the Keeper on whose beat the Meet is held.

Opposite: Marsh gentian *Gentiana pneumonanthe.* Clockwise from top left: Apple *Malus domestica agg.* Sloe *Prunus spinosa.* Oak *Quercus robu.* Apple *Malus domestica agg.* Sweet chestnut *Castanea sativa.* Beech *Fagus sylvatica.*

Red Deer Rut

By tradition the red deer rut has always seemed to be on Ober Plain watched and followed by hundreds of photographers. Understandably the deer move off but nobody seemed to know where the year I was there. There was a big crop of acorns and beech mast that meant the hinds would likely be in the woods and the stags with them.

It took me quite some days to find the hinds but then I heard the 'roaring' in the woods. Giant, as he is known, had almost all the hinds in the area. As his working day unfolded in front of my camera I realised with wonder and surprise how complex his day was. He was having a challenging time, not only because he was being followed by other stags trying to take his many hinds from him, but because

of all the black Labradors that were bothering him. I was shocked by how many people take their dog for a walk off the lead and then never give a thought as to where it is. It is easy to see why there are fatalities among deer and dogs. Deer see dogs as a threat and act accordingly, but it is very often the deer that gets injured.

I try to photograph a working animal in the same way that I would photograph a human being at work. I was attracted to the character in Giant's face in the same way as I would be to a human's. I tried to look into him rather than at him. So I spent four whole days with this stag, deep in the woods. Mostly I stood behind or up trees and, above all, ensured I was never in his way. I travelled deep into the woods

with him and his hinds and became completely lost. Occasionally he would look up and acknowledge me but on the whole he ignored me. He seemed to know when the light was working for me. I was completely alone with the herd. It was a real privilege to have such a close encounter with a wild stag.

Opposite: Red stag hoping for success with this hind. Above: Red stag proudly roaring among his hinds. Overleaf: Red stags challenging one another's strengths.

Previous spread: Red stag
chasing his hinds during
the rut, full of hope.
Below: A young opportunist
red stag that hopes to steal
some of the hinds.
Opposite top: Ever watchful,
the red stag looks round
while guarding his hinds.
Opposite bottom: Among
all the activity of the rut,
a hind feeds her calf.

Autumn

Fallow Rut

Like the red deer rut the fallow rut attracts photographers and so, with the help of the Keepers, I looked for areas that most would not think of. The best photographs always seem to be through thick woods and under the trees! There the bucks are 'groaning' on their established 'stands' with many does taking their pick. However by staying in one place for hours, suddenly a beautiful buck looking for does can appear out of the trees or bracken looking magnificent.

Opposite: A fallow buck during the rut.
Above: A fallow buck passing another Forest dweller.

Below: A fallow buck on his rutting stand under the trees groaning to attract does gets some definite success.
Opposite top: A 'spent' fallow buck sits down while a Forest pony eats its way around him.
Opposite bottom: A fallow buck on his rutting stand assessing his situation.

Autumn

Opposite: A fallow buck
during the rutting season.
Above: Fallow bucks
competing for the does.

Sika Rut

Top: A young sika stag during the rut.
Bottom: A sika hind dashes through the undergrowth during the rut.
Opposite: A sika hind alert during the rut.

The sika rut is probably the most difficult to photograph. To me it seemed frenetic with stags dashing here and there with the hinds doing the same. Very near by you can hear the stags whistling so for me the best way was to stay in one place and see what came by. Whenever I saw a hind I knew a stag would be close behind her.

Autumn

Opposite top: A sika stag that has been wallowing in mud and his own urine to make himself attractive to hinds.
Opposite bottom: A sika stag coming through the bracken looking for hinds.
Above: Sika stag.
Overleaf: Sika stag stealthily moves through the bracken in his search for hinds.

In the midst *of* life we are *in* death

The two fallow bucks tied together by the antlers with netting. They look up through the bracken and heather, but it was impossible for the Keepers to shoot them there because there was a footpath behind them.

The harsh reality in the world of nature is that it can be a very unforgiving environment.

Deer are normally cautious and wary – watching for abnormal movement, scenting the air, checking for the smell of danger. The females give the impression of being more alert than the males. This tragic event seems to confirm that. During the hours of darkness and on a full stomach, the male deer seem to feel secure and become inquisitive. Very often they feast on Commoners' holdings where the pickings are more rewarding.

Hay nets are often tied to a convenient fence post or a low branch. When they are empty the male deer treat them like play objects. Occasionally the antlers become entangled. The buck breaks free with the hay net still in his antlers, and escapes back on to the Forest where local people spot him and the reports come back to the beat Keeper. In this case Keeper Tim Creed searched and found nothing. A day or two later he received another report from a horse rider that two bucks had become entangled by the hay net in their antlers. This was not surprising because during the rutting season the bucks would naturally spar and the netting would tie them together. At the time Keeper Tim Creed was in the company of Keeper Graham Wilson and they were quickly on the scene. With the aid of Tim's dog Fran, after a few hours the bucks were found in an area of high heather and gorse. The deer were quickly dispatched. Both had to be dispatched at the same

time, or one could have gone off dragging the other. Two Keepers were needed for the job, but it was not an easy task for the Keepers because there were many walkers in the area. They were then examined and it was found that one deer had suffered a broken leg during its ordeal. The bucks were both emaciated from their experience and would not have survived the winter. Without Fran the ordeal of the bucks would have lasted a lot longer.

This is an example of the harsh reality of life in the wild.

This is not the only misfortune that can befall bucks during the rut: Will Day was out laying a trail for the New Forest Hounds when he came across a buck who couldn't stand and seemed to have gone

blind. He was probably dehydrated from excessive rutting. He called local Keeper Alan Stride who arrived within five minutes and put the animal out of its misery. If the buck had been left he would have died from exposure and it would not have been possible to treat a large wild animal in pain.

Clockwise from top left: The fallow bucks briefly raise their heads while trying to disentangle themselves from each other. Keepers Tim Creed (left) and Graham Wilson search for the fallow bucks. Tim Creed's dog Fran justly pleased with herself once the ordeal is over. Tim Creed walks ahead of Graham Wilson looking for the fallow bucks while also listening for any movement.

Fungi

Fungi have been recorded in the New Forest for over a century, with a significant increase in the last 30 years. A great richness of species, including rare and endangered ones with probably many others yet to be discovered, make it mycologically very significant.

The varied geology, topography and subsequent land use or non disturbance of the sandy gravels which predominate, with important areas of estuarine clays in the south (where calciferous fungi can be found), are all rare qualities in a comparatively small region. Long established pasture woodland with mature trees and decaying wood, grassland and heathland is all grazed by Commoners' livestock, interspersed by coniferous plantations. This contributes to make it a nationally assessed Important Fungal Area with the 'highest importance for fungi achievable in this country'. It is also designated as a Site of Special Scientific Interest and a Special Area of Conservation.

Because the New Forest is easily accessible to all, it is now having to cope with huge pressures from people. Unfortunately the picking of fungi has been stimulated and encouraged by the media, particularly television and celebrity chefs, on an increasing scale since the 1990s. People are attracted to fungi for various reasons: some collect on a commercial scale to sell, others for their own culinary use (with a risk of poisoning if incorrectly identified), some to just admire or photograph, and the curious to join fungi

Clockwise from top left: Beechwood sickener *Russula nobilis*. False deathcap *Amanita citrina*. Orange aak bolete *Leccinum aurantiacum*. Devil's fingers *Clathrus archeri*.

Top: Sara Cadbury
holding a spindleshank
Collybia fusipes.
Middle: Blusher *Amanita
rubescens*.
Bottom: Horse mushroom
Agaricus arvensis.

Clockwise from top left:
Honey fungus *Armillaria
mellea*. Sulphur tuft
Hypholoma fasciculare.
The flirt *Russula vesca*.
Bay bolete *Leccinum
cyaneobasileucum*. Bay
bolete *Bolitus badius*.
Hypholoma subericaeoides.
Oyster mushroom
Pleurotus ostreatus.
Chicken of the woods
Laetiporus sulphureus.

forays led by a mycologist, to learn more about them. Mycologists record the fungi to enter them onto a national database and publish detailed survey work.

Commercial collecting was banned by the Department for Environment, Food & Rural Affairs in 1998 under the Theft Act, and the Forestry Commission (as land manager) is also able to provide protection under a local byelaw. Recently the New Forest Keepers have been given the responsibility of robustly controlling commercial picking and limiting the general public to collecting a small amount.

Fungi add to the biodiversity and are an essential part of the fragile ecosystem, with a special symbiotic relationship with trees to the benefit of all. They provide food for some animals and many insects rely on them to complete their lifecycles. Rare and threatened species, although legally protected, are being collected, and disturbance to wildlife and ground trampling are serious issues. Scientific research is being held up and an good amenity value for everyone, is being spoiled.

As it is now considered unacceptable to collect wild flowers, butterflies and birds' eggs, etc., so the colleciton of fungi in the New Forest should be the same. Collecting is having a negative environmental impact on an important area. There is a requirement for us to move from gastronomic enjoyment to one of visual appreciation and care of the environment. *Sara Cadbury* New Forest Mycologist

Clockwise from top left: Fly agaric *Amanita muscaria*. **Fly agaric** *Amanita muscaria*. **Southern bracket** *Ganoderma australe*. *Marasmiellus candidus*. **False deathcap** *Amanita citrina*.

Clockwise from top left:
Fly agaric *Amanita muscaria*.
Spectacular rustgill
Gymnopilus junonius. *Bolitus
species*. Butter cap *Collybia
butyracea*. Humpback
brittlegill *Russula caerulea*.
Clouded funnel *Clitocybe
nebularis*.

Clockwise from top left:
Fly agaric *Amanita
muscaria*. Humpback
brittlegill *Russula
caerulea*. Brown rollrim
Paxillus involutus. Parasol
Macrolepiota procera.
Amethyst deceiver *Laccaria
amethystina*.
Bay bolete *Bolitus badius*.

The Noctule *and* Natterer's Bats

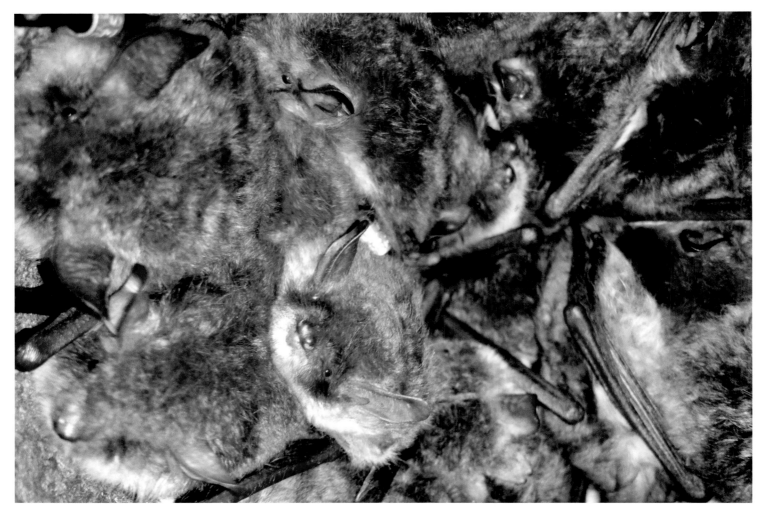

The New Forest is a stronghold for bats and probably 13 out of the 18 UK species can be found here. Three of them are particularly rare: Greater Horseshoe and the tree roosting Bechstein's and Barbastelle.

As the only flying mammal in the world, bats are a vital part of our native wildlife. Their presence indicates a healthy environment so their future is directly linked to our own quality of life. Fossil evidence of mammals similar to bats dates back over 50 million years. The UK's largest bat is the Noctule, with a wingspan of 33-45cm. The Noctule bat mates from August through to October. Male and female bats can store sperm for up to seven months without the sperm losing their fertilising capacity.

The gestation period is 70 to 73 days with a single offspring being born in June or July. The maximum age recorded in Europe is 12 years.

A baby bat is called a 'pup'. Bats usually produce one offspring a year. This means bat populations cannot rebuild their numbers quickly and are sensitive to harmful impacts. Pups can fly four to five weeks after they are born. The collective name for a group of bats is a 'colony'. Their places of rest are known as 'roosts' and are protected by law. Bats will use a number of roost sites according to the time of year. Common roosts for bats are caves, trees and buildings in the eaves, roofs or cellars.

Bats are protected by law because their numbers have decreased so dramatically.

The first recorded Natterer's bat maternity roost in a New Forest bat box.

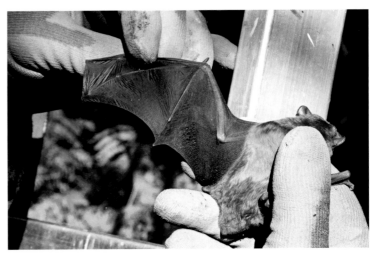

New Forest Keepers Howard Taylor and Tim Creed were doing their bat survey to try to locate the two rare Bechstein's and Barbastelle species. There is a historic record of Beckstein's bat recorded at this location. One was submitted to the National History Museum back in Victorian times.

The Forestry Commission was doing the work, originally in conjunction with the Vincent Wildlife Trust. Surveys are done from spring through to October. These surveys cannot be done without a licence and the Forestry Commission insists that all bat workers have a Rabies inoculation.

This particular survey had approximately 50 boxes that were checked once a month. As the quality of radio telemetry tracking progresses, bat boxes are used less often now. This particular survey was started 20 years ago when there was no radio tracking technology small enough for bats.

On this occasion Howard and Tim found Natterer's bats and Noctule bats. In fact that day they found the first recorded Natterer's bat maternity roost in a New Forest bat box. You can see the juvenile bats inside the box.

The wings are examined for fractures, holes, tears or bleeds in the membrane; foreign bodies; dullness caused by dehydration or dust; ectoparasites/ticks; ulceration and/or stickiness or contamination of the membrane; ossification of the bones to help estimate age; and the general condition of the bat, such as if it is pregnant or undernourished.

Permits
and
Licences

The Forestry Commission is responsible for managing the Crown lands in the New Forest. It has to balance the needs of people, nature and business. Jayne Albery, the Commission's Recreation Officer, receives several thousand requests for permits and licences every year. All this activity has to be assessed against conservation and ecology requirements, the needs of other forest users, and of course in the context of the working Forest.

The New Forest is unique. It is a Site of Special Scientific Interest, a Special Area of Conservation, Special Protection Area for Birds and also a Ramsar site (a wetland of international importance). It is safeguarded by the European Union Habitats Directive and is governed by a complex set of New Forest Acts and Forestry Commission bylaws.

The wildlife habitats – from extensive wet and dry heathlands and grasslands, to valley mires, ancient pastures and enclosed woodland – must be protected. Plus of course the protected species such as the nightjar, wild gladioli, southern damselfly and honey buzzard. All these need an extra special level of protection against 13.5 million day-trippers, and a million overnight stays, because it really is a special resource.

Jayne Albery, with Keepers Alan Stride and Jonathan Cook, casually observes the participants of a ride and drive event cooling off in the river.

Top: Jayne Albery, Forestry Commission's Recreation Officer, checks the wellbeing of the huskies that are about to race.
Middle: The start of a husky race that is permitted under licence to take part at an agreed location on the Forest.

Winter

Every mile is two in winter.
George Herbert

Winter seems a quieter time of year but the Keepers still have much work to do.

The smell of damp leaves is a reminder of the changing seasons. The misty mornings and low setting sun herald the winter days with long nights and short days. The commoning Keepers have made their hay that is safely stored.

The New Forest has 193,000 acres of ancient woodland, open expanses of heathland with sparkling streams, and coastlines. The beautiful ice-tinged deciduous trees stand proudly on the Forest, the frosty blue skies contrast with the beautiful copper leaves. Winter in the New Forest is truly a spectacular sight to see. It has always been a good time to look at the shape of some of the New Forest's ancient trees when they aren't in full leaf.

Heywood Sumner, doyen of New Forest landscape writers, said in the last century 'that winter perambulations in the forest have a special charm. The morning light streaming through the near-barren canopy allows the woodland's structure to be seen most clearly. Shapes are discovered that have been hidden for many months. The oaks have lost almost all of their lower leaves. Those still held high up give the topmost branches a bronze halo when the sun catches them. At this season, and in this atmosphere, this wood exudes enchantment. I sense eyes watching me and, though I turn slowly, see only

the white rump of the deer as it slips silently away.'

In the run up to Christmas the Keepers help with the selling of Christmas trees, which gives them the chance to talk to the locals in a relaxed and festive atmosphere. Then of course there is the Boxing Day Point to Point that is the most important event in the commoning year. The start is kept secret until just before the race, but the Keeper over whose beat it runs must know of course!

The carefully structured deer cull continues on from late autumn. The Keepers are all up very early and in their high seats, even before the dog walkers come out. Or so they hope.

In late winter if the weather has been harsh, holly is cut for food, which is known as pollarding. This is done in the Ancient Ornamental Woodlands frequented by deer and ponies alike.

Previous spread: Red deer in winter.
Left: Tim Creed and Sandy Shore sell Christmas trees to the public. Sandy Shore took over Tim Creed's beat when he retired in 2015.
Opposite top: Beech leaves in the frost.
Opposite bottom: Red hinds on a cold morning.

Deer Management

Howard Taylor (left) and Tim Creed prepare for a morning shoot.

Deer are culled to prevent too large a population because there are no longer any natural predators in the UK such as wolves or lynxes.

As large herbivores they can dramatically affect populations of rare butterflies by grazing and browsing the butterfly (caterpillar) food plants, as well as the food plants of many other insects. They will also maraud off of the Forest onto private land causing crop and garden damage. The deer themselves suffer at large population densities due to greater numbers of parasites and disease. Also, in years of a hard winter deer will die under these conditions. Kept at the correct population density the deer are fit and healthy and they are in balance with their environment.

As a basis for managing deer, the most important requirement is knowledge of the population size. The New Forest Keepers all do a count on their beat and report back to Head Keeper Andy Page. While annual cull targets are used as a tool to manage deer towards a target population, it is recognised that these targets are less important than the resultant condition of the habitat and the deer themselves. Various information is taken into account when setting cull targets. These may include: computer modelling of the population, field observations, stakeholder feedback, damage assessments and the health of the deer. The Keepers who use high velocity rifles from high seats undertake the cull. Each keeper is a marksman and trained with the firearm.

Deer are all gralloched within an hour of shooting in the field at the place they are shot. The green waste (stomach, small and large intestines and the chain of glands) is visibly checked for disease and abnormalities. It is then left behind a tree for the many Forest dwellers that would consider this a bonus feast. It is natural recycling.

Clockwise from top left: Howard and Tim discuss their plan. Tim sets off with his dog Fran. Howard has had success and extracts a fallow deer from where it fell. Howard observes something and prepares to shoot.

Winter

Opposite: Fallow bucks.
Top: Tim Creed in a high seat on observation before the deer cull.
Bottom: Tim extracts the deer that he has just shot back to a collection point.

Winter

Opposite: Matthew Davies,
whose beat is in the north
of the Forest, grallochs a
deer that he has just shot.
The trail of blood is from
a successful shot through
the heart.
Below: Matthew loads
the deer into the back
of his vehicle.

Clockwise from top left: Keepers (left to right) Howard Taylor, Graham Wilson, Jonathan Cook and Robert Colin-Stokes (now in a different Forestry Commission job) stop for a debrief after a team shoot. Beat partners Alan Stride (left) and Patrick Cook extracting one of the deer that they shot that day. Alan Stride grallochs a deer that he has just shot. This always happens within an hour of shooting. Maarten Ledeboer uses a deer call.

The green waste (stomach, small and large intestines and the chain of glands) having been visibly checked for disease and abnormalities, is then left behind a tree for the many hungry Forest dwellers. It is natural recycling. Overleaf: Patrick Cook examines a culled deer.

Deer
Larder

Once the carcass has been loaded into the back of the Keeper's vehicle it doesn't touch the ground again. It is taken to the Forestry Commission's modern automated larder where it is put on a winch and the other glands, heart, liver and lungs and checked for abnormalities.

The carcasses are stored at not less than 4 degrees centigrade until a suitable amount have built up for one of Game dealers to collect for final butchering and processing to go to the consumer. About every three years the game dealers tender to buy the New Forest venison. Wild venison is very healthy low cholesterol meat. You cannot get anything more free range and organic because deer living wild in the woods do not have any artificial feeding.

After a team shoot, the Keepers work quickly in the Larder to prepare the carcasses for the chill room.

Clockwise from top left:
Carcasses in the back of
a Keeper's vehicle, just
returned from a stalk.
Matt Davies checks his
knife before starting work.
Maarten Ledeboer cleans
out the back of his vehicle.
Alan Stride (left) and
Patrick Cook preparing
two carcasses.

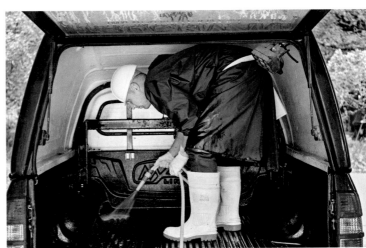

Top: Jonathan Cook
making a final examination
of a prepared carcass.
Middle: Patrick Cook
ensuring that the prepared
carcasses are stored
correctly in the chill room.

Top: A morning's work.
Left: Every deer carcass
has a detailed label to
ensure that it is traceable.

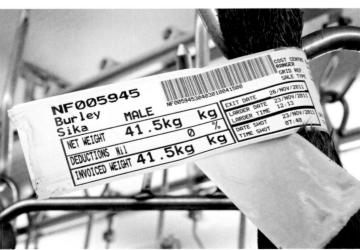

Top: A red hind demonstrates her versatility at being able to browse the ivy.
Bottom: In harsh weather conditions holly is pollarded (cut) as a supplementary feed.

Above: Red deer in the woods on a sunny winter's morning.
Overleaf: A proud sika stag with his hinds of different ages.

Winter

Opposite: A startled
muntjac doe races through
the undergrowth.
Below: Sika stag with
two hinds.
Overleaf: On a cold
and frosty morning
the red deer stand still.

Hunting
on the
New Forest

"He made large forests for the deer and enacted laws therewith, so that whoever killed a hart or a hind should be killed."
Anglo Saxon Chronicle 1087 referring to William The Conqueror.

It could be argued that the New Forest owes its very existence to hunting. Historically, the word 'forest' referred to a royal hunting area in which certain animals, like deer, would have been protected by law. The New Forest was William The Conqueror's first hunting Forest in all England and it was where he hunted 'beasts of the chase' for enjoyment and food. Even the fallow deer (Dama dama) for which the New Forest is famous, and where they were still hunted up until 1997,

probably owe their existence in Britain to hunting (venison literally means 'the meat of the hunt').

The Forestry Commission has always allowed hunting over its lands in the New Forest where it has been traditionally carried on. Trail hunting continues in the New Forest under License granted by the Deputy Surveyor and is subject to strictly enforced conditions. In July 1997, after over 900 years, the New Forest Buckhounds stopped hunting fallow bucks.

**Previous spread: Red stag moves into the sunlight on a cold morning.
Above: The New Forest Hounds.**

Top: The Master warms himself with a little whisky before a long day's hunting.
Middle: Huntsman Michael Woodhouse at the Meet.
Bottom: Looking for a trail.
Overleaf: Huntsman Michael Woodhouse takes his hounds towards the woods to find a trail.

The New Forest Hounds

The New Forest Hounds were put on a formal footing in 1780. Mr H V Gilbert was the first Master.

The New Forest Hunt Club was instituted in 1789 for the purpose of hunting the New Forest Country. The Lord Warden of the New Forest (the Duke of Gloucester) nominated Mr Gilbert's hounds to be the established pack of the country, in succession to his own, with prior rights to hunt the New Forest. In season 1789-1790 they became a subscription pack under the New Forest Hunt Club, Mr Gilbert remained in office as Master until 1800.

These hounds still meet twice a week across the Forest during the season from September to April.

Since the Hunting Act in 2004 a trail has obviously been hunted. The New Forest Hounds hunt within the Law.

It used to be the duty of the New Forest Keepers to stop large earths (foxholes) on the morning of the Hunt. The New Forest Keepers did not control the fox population, although the Crown Office could not be seen to be permitting large numbers of foxes to the detriment of their neighbours. The New Forest Hounds fulfilled the role at no expense to the Crown Administration!

Today, the joint Masters and the hunt club employ staff to hunt hounds, and run the affairs of the hunt through a committee rather than a Mastership, which is slightly unusual. Traditionally the Mastership of a hunt takes financial responsibility

Hounds pour out of their kennels eager for exercise.

During the summer Huntsman Michael Woodhouse exercises his hounds on a bicycle.

for the hunt, personally injecting funds to support the hunt club as required. However the modern world produces fewer individuals able (or willing) to take this responsibility, so it was decided in the year 2000 to become a committee pack. Masters of Fox Hounds Association rules still stipulate that a hunt must have a nominated master(s), and the work of the Mastership must still be done. The New Forest Hounds do therefore still have two Masters, but the financial burden of the hunt is borne by the Hunt Club through the committee.

It is good to see that a long established Forest tradition is still going strong. The social side of Forest life is still flourishing round many social events.

The New Forest Beagles

Captain Keith Gladstone, Master of the Ringwood Beagles in 1920, was able to establish the New Forest Beagles with priceless strains of beagle bloodlines.

This pack had been carefully bred by their former Master the late Sir Frederick Fitz Wygram and were considered one of the hardest working and best-looking packs in the country. Fred Day lent his Country (the land over which he was licensed to hunt) to Captain Gladstone and, with his brother Ernest, whipped in for him. During this time fine sport was shown and the pack had an excellent reputation. A stallion hound, Ringwood Merlin, was said to have made five packs of Beagles and, later, the stallion hound New Forest Harbourer was in big demand.

In 1928 Captain Gladstone retired. A Committee was formed and the pack was taken over and became a subscription pack. New kennels were built at Bartley where they still remain. Mr Ernest Day was established as Master and Huntsman, and remained in this position until he retired in 1950. Thus, the New Forest Beagles began.

During the Second World War the pack was reduced and a small pack was kept going, hunting only on Saturdays. Ernest Day's cousin, Bryan Day, who had whipped in, started to hunt them and became Joint Master in 1946. At the end of hostilities he re-built the pack from the valuable strains which had been preserved. After 26 years he retired and was succeeded by his son Michael who had become

Opposite: Beagles waiting for instructions.
Top: Whipper in Jon Cleal.
Middle: Huntsman Tina Bick, in her 20th Season as Huntsman, with her 'jelly dog' beagles demonstrating how much they love her.
Bottom: Tina Bick with her beagles always gets extremely muddy.

Joint Master in 1976. He retired in 1977, ending an unbroken run of the Day family as Masters for over 40 years. The Day family, through the generations, have been stalwarts of the Hounds.

Today there is a very happy team with the hounds and supporters in good heart.

The Beagles still hunt the Forest, although only once a week and of course only a trail. The change to trail hunting as a result of the 2004 Hunting Act was difficult at first, but hounds have adapted since and work well in the field making it a fine spectacle for the hunt follower. Beagles are exciting little hounds known as 'jelly dogs'. They are always anxious, busy and ready to hunt. They are very, very affectionate and so are the perfect way to introduce a child to hounds.

As with the New Forest Hounds, there is a healthy social side helping to maintain that wonderful Forest tradition.

Opposite and above: New
Forest Beagles hunting a
trail on the New Forest.
Left: Beagles eager to come
out of their trailer for a
day's trail hunting.

Rabbit Control Beagles *and* Ferrets

The need for Rabbit control varies from season to season. They are usually widespread throughout the New Forest although occasionally there are surprisingly few. The outbreak of the Myxomatosis virus in early 1950's reduced the rabbit population, but it has recovered well in the Forest and numbers are rapidly increasing due to their breeding habits and their increasing immunity to Myxomatosis. There is another 'rabbit' virus that has appeared with distastrous consequences known as the 'Chinese Disease'.

They can be seen at any time of day or night grazing on the Forest eating a wide range of vegetation. They live in warrens, where they give birth to litters of up to seven young, sometimes 4 to 5 times a year. These newborn rabbits (kittens) are blind and naked at birth, but they grow rapidly and are weaned at about a month old.

They are mischievous animals and like to take the tops of freshly planted trees. The tell tale sign is that the cut is at a 45 degree angle like secateurs. Some trees are more vulnerable than others. They do the most damage when vegetation growth is at its lowest and they are hungry. When there is snow or ice around they take the bark off trees. A lot of rabbits can do a lot of damage to a freshly planted plantation of trees or to private gardens.

They are vulnerable to the larger raptors and are the favourite food of buzzards, but on the whole the population has to be controlled. Some years ago

Opposite: Ian Young sets out with his own beagles to flush out rabbits that are damaging freshly planted trees and the plants in gardens.
Above: Ian Young coming through the woods with one of his own beagles.
Left: Ian back home with his beagles.

Ian Young prepares to catch
more rabbits with his
Ferrets. He puts the ferret
down the rabbit hole and
the rabbit rushes out into
the purse nets that he has
put over the holes. He also
has a long net carefully laid
out in strategic positions
to block escape routes.
Opposite: Ian Young
returning home, carrying
his ferret box, after a
successful day.

New
Forest
Falconry

The New Forest has two falconry clubs that share the Hunt with Hawks licence, using alternate weekends. Paul Manning of Amews Falconry is a member of the Wessex Falconry & Hampshire Hawking Club.

'Falconry in this area pre-dates the establishment of the New Forest in 1079, so there has been an unbroken heritage of falconry here. From the late 11th century falconry rose to become the country's pre-eminent pastime, first for the ruling classes and then the wider population. This popularity was matched in almost all cultures around the world, from China, Japan and Korea through the Middle East and India to Europe and Scandinavia.

'This has recently been acknowledged by UNESCO, who in 2010 designated falconry a world heritage sport for its contribution to the cooperation and understanding between diverse nations and cultures.

'Our club meets early Saturday morning every other week from November to February as part of the Forestry Commission's pest control programme. Mainly hunting rabbits using ferrets, dogs and, of course, hawks, we practise this ancient sport exactly as it has been practised here for a thousand years.' The relevant beat Keeper is always informed.

Graham Reeves is a member of the Hampshire Falconry Association.

'All the birds used in falconry are captive bred and initially birds were very difficult and expensive to obtain. At first the majority of members flew

Mike Riley of the Wessex Falconry & Hampshire Hawking Club.

red-tailed hawks or common buzzards, but now the harris hawk has become the bird of choice. These birds originate from the deserts of the southern states of the USA and throughout South America. Unusually for birds of prey, they live in extended family groups which cooperate when hunting.'

Gerald Lascelles – Deputy Surveyor of the New Forest 1880-1914 – was instrumental in keeping the sport of falconry alive in Britain. In 1872 he became Secretary of the 'Old Hawking Club' and he held the position for 44 years.

Controlled Burning

The heathlands of the New Forest that are often referred to as the Open Forest cover approximately 18,000 hectares. The Open Forest is made up of a variety of habitats from areas of dry heath to wet valley mires. In order to maintain its traditional character and value for the grazing of commoning stock there is an extensive Open Forest management programme that includes controlled burning. The burning of gorse and heather encourages new growth that is beneficial to a variety of flora and fauna, and creates food for commoning stock. It also results in a mosaic of different aged habitats that create effective fire breaks to protect large areas of heathland, woodland and private property from wildfire.

Controlled burning is undertaken in the late winter and almost exclusively in February and March but is entirely weather dependant. The areas for treatment are derived from a series of field visits conducted the previous summer between representatives from the Forestry Commission, Natural England and the Commoners and Verderers. Selected areas are chosen to regenerate and rejuvenate older or more senescent stands of heather and gorse. Local conservation issues are discussed and where necessary modifications to treatment practices are made. Annual treatment acreage can vary between 600 and 1100 acres across the whole Forest and can number around 130 separate treatment areas. Some sites are cut with a tractor-mounted flail or mulcher while others are

Keepers Graham Wilson (left) and Tim Creed work together. Graham is blowing out the flame on his paraffin burner and Tim is hosing the ground to ensure the flame does not burn with ferocity.

Clockwise from top left:
Andy Shore does a lot of
the controlled burning.
Howard Taylor at the end of
a successful day's burning.
Ian Young frequently
works with Andy Shore.
Overleaf: Graham Wilson
lights the heather behind
a spray of water from the
bowser which quells the
ferocity of the flames.

burned in the traditional way using skilled teams of 4 to 6 people. All burn sites are traced round with a tractor-mounted flail to assist safety during the actual burning operation. Some heather sites are cut and baled by contractors to provide natural material for use in mire and stream restoration projects.

It also has one additional benefit that no other type of heathland management, including cutting or swiping, can provide and that is the reduction of ticks and the risk of Lymes Disease. An old traditional benefit of controlled burning, but not practised today, was the harvesting by the Commoners of the 'blackjacks' – the burnt holly and gorse stems – to sell as firewood. Today the only indications of blackjacks are curious foals with blackened zebra-like stripes on their haunches and faces.

Just before the last war there were great conflicts between the Commoners and the Forestry Commission over the extent of the burning programme. Commoners felt that insufficient land had been burned so they ran their own unofficial parallel programme. The Commission responded by further severe cuts in the burns as punishment. Today things are much more civilised with both sides keen to cooperate. Anyway, as one old Commoner remarked – there is very little point in setting fire to the Forest these days because the Commission's fire fighting teams are so fast and efficient.

Commoning Keepers

The Crown Lands of the New Forest are regulated by the Verderers under the various New Forest Acts of 1877, 1949, 1964 and 1970. The New Forest is effectively a giant 60,000-acre farmer's field, shared by 700 smallholders who we call Commoners. The Verderers employ five Agisters who, on horseback, supervise the condition of the agricultural grazing stock: the iconic New Forest pony, the cattle herds, and the donkeys and pigs.

The Verderers rely on effective land management of the New Forest Crown Lands by the Forestry Commission, and the key people in this are the Crown Keepers, who do much more than simply manage the deer population. They are the eyes and ears, effectively our forest policemen, solving problems in real time as they arise, alerting the various forest bodies when a damaging trend or ecological problem is developing and helping to resolve encroachments.

The Keepers have a level of knowledge and skill which is critical to the good condition of the New Forest. They all have individual expertise in diverse subjects such as deer management, birds or fish, which is an invaluable resource. Additionally, many of the Keepers are also Commoners, practising the ancient form of pastoral farming which has created the beautiful New Forest landscape. In grazing their ponies and cattle on the commons lands, using their occupation of Crown Freehold, it provides the link with our Agisters, so important for the seamless

Previous spread: A burn site when the work is over shows the seedling pine has been successfully burned which avoids its encroachment on to the heathland.
Above: Several of the Keepers are Commoners. Graham Wilson runs cattle on the Forest that have to be TB tested by a vet with the Agister present.

Top: Patrick Cook runs ponies and cattle on the Forest and puts his pig out with her piglets during the annual pannage season. (Pigs eat the acorns, which helps to save the ponies and cattle, who can fall ill from the toxic tannin they contain.

Middle: Agister Mike Lovell received an emergency call about a pony stuck in a ditch while he was helping with the TB testing of Graham Wilson's cattle. Graham went along to help with pulling the pony out of the ditch. The Keepers and Agisters frequently work together on Forest matters.

Bottom: Ian Young runs ponies on the Forest and is seen here bringing them on to his holding.

management of this internationally important area and unique system of farming.

I am so pleased that the Crown Keepers of the New Forest are being recognised by the publication of this brilliant book, and I look forward to the continuation of their good work for generations to come.
Dominic May Official Verderer of the New Forest

The Verderers' Court dates back to medieval times. The court consists of ten Verderers: five are elected and five are appointed. The five elected Verderers must all be Commoners. The official Verderer, who presides over all, is appointed by Her Majesty the Queen. The Verderers employ the five Agisters who look after the Commoners' stock on the Forest.

A Brief History *of the* Keepers *of the* New Forest

Richard Reeves New Forest Historian

The Keepers of the New Forest can trace their origins to the creation of the New Forest by William the Conqueror. The Domesday Survey ordered by that king contains the earliest references to Foresters on the New Forest. In medieval times the Keepers were known as Foresters and forests were areas of land over which forest law applied. As such, once an area was designated a forest, Foresters were required to look after it and enforce the forest laws.

The earliest recorded Foresters were Foresters of Fee, a designation which indicates that the post was hereditary, as well as attached to specific land holdings which were themselves associated with specific areas of the forest known as Bailiwicks and over which each Forester had jurisdiction. For example, the de Lyndhurst family held the Manor of Lyndhurst and were Foresters for the Bailiwick of Lyndhurst.

Being men of status, the Foresters of Fee undertook their duties by means of deputies known as Foot Foresters and Riding Foresters. These under-Foresters would be responsible for the enforcement of forest laws, presenting offences at the forest courts, looking after the beasts of the Forest and the habitats in which they lived, overseeing the use of Forest land by the Commoners, collecting certain payments for the exercise of common rights and bringing in the Forest stock at the drifts. This continued to be the management regime until the late-13th century.

In the mid-13th century, King Henry III granted the New Forest to his son Edward (later King Edward I) who in turn passed it to his consort Eleanor of Castile. She was to rearrange the New Forest's administrative hierarchy to maximise the income she could derive from the Forest. This was done, circa 1270, by way of a three-way land exchange, whereby she acquired the stewardship of the Forest and the Manor of Lyndhurst with its associated Bailiwick. Later, in 1276, she was to acquire control over the other bailiwicks by way of a somewhat loaded court action against the Foresters of Fee. With this the link between landholdings and their associated bailiwicks was broken, while the large Bailiwick of Lyndhurst was subdivided. This apparently created a need for lodges to accommodate the Foresters, who were now appointed by the Stewards of the Forest on behalf of the Crown; the post of Forester had ceased to be a hereditary one.

The Forest remained in the Queen's dower until 1354, in which year King Edward III exchanged lands with his wife Philippa of Hainault to bring the Forest under his control. Soon after this he was to upgrade certain properties on the Forest, including Foresters' lodges, as basis for his hunting parties; a course of action followed by his grandson King Richard II. It is clear the Foresters would have had a key role to play in the King's hunting trips and coincidentally the earliest book on hunting in English, *Master of the Game*, was a translation from a French source, with additions, by Edward Langley, 2nd Duke of York.

Alice Gulliver in 1951 outside her home, Bramshaw Wood Cottage. Her son Keeper Willy, now retired, was an Under Keeper at the time living at home. He used to cycle from Bramshaw Wood to Burley every day and he came across an orphan fallow fawn whose mother was dead. He brought the fawn home for his own mother to look after. (Note: today it is recognised good practice if you find a fawn to leave it where it is for 12 hours in case the mother is nearby.)

Clockwise from top left: George Blake, Head Keeper at Pipers Wait, takes aim at a buck in the mid-1940s. George Blake collecting beech nuts with a colleague, 1920. George Blake training pupils of the Foresters' School at Burley on what to do with the beech nuts, 1920.

He was Justice in Eyre of the Forests, Trent South, and also held the chief post in the New Forest, that of Lord Warden. As such the additions he made to the French original may well have derived in part from knowledge he gained from his post in the New Forest.

The next major event to impact upon the Foresters, though not at first directly, was the introduction of Exchequer officers with a management interest in the forests. An office was first introduced for wood sales during the reign of King Henry VII and this was fully developed under King Henry VIII leading to the post of Surveyor General of Woods – one for lands north of the River Trent and one for lands to the south. Beneath this position were Deputy Surveyors, responsible for each county or group of counties, and in later times each forest or group of forests. This created a dual management regime for the forests, one that was often in dispute, and which became known as the 'Divisium Imperium'. The new regime was soon to have a direct impact on the Foresters, who in 1584 were deprived of their claim to all fallen wood and timber within their respective bailiwicks, though they received payment in lieu thereof.

This early rise in silvicultural interest was paralleled by a reorganisation of the Foresters' lodges. The old medieval lodges were replaced by a suite of new lodges which differed from the earlier ones by the addition of large enclosed paddocks. Here the Foresters would bring browsewood from

pollarded trees to feed the deer, free from competition with the commonable stock of local inhabitants. Originally there appears to have been one lodge per bailiwick but over time more were added and early in the reign of King James I a review was undertaken and a number of new lodges were ordered to be built. This led to the subdivision of the larger bailiwicks into two or three walks. Around this time new terminology arose, so that the Chief Forester in charge of each bailiwick became known as a Head Keeper, and the Under Forester in charge of each walk was known as the Under Keeper, though court records often continued to use the old terminology.

Under King James I further restrictions as to the protection of timber also came into force, which were to affect the Keepers. These included restrictions as to cutting browsewood. When the primary forest court visited the Forest in 1635 a number of Keepers fell foul of the new regulations, being found to have cut unnecessary browsewood for the deer. This probably had more to do with financial interests than any particular care for the deer in their charge, for the Keepers were permitted to sell the browsewood once the deer had stripped the bark, buds and leaves from the boughs. Such traversing of the trusts reposed in the Keepers and other forest officers was common, for the isolated places in which they operated provided great facilities and much in the way of temptation.

In 1669, three experimental inclosures of land for the raising of timber were ordered and while this

experiment largely failed more were to follow. In 1698, an Act of Parliament was passed for the inclosure of land within the New Forest to provide timber for the Navy. Within a few years a number of parcels of land had been inclosed and fenced to keep both commonable stock and deer out. This marked the point at which the rise of silvicultural really got under way and the parallel management systems of the Forest found themselves coming to blows with increasing regularity. While the Keepers might be presumed to have stood in opposition to the new inclosures, they were also to benefit – for a short time at least – as the plantations made in the 1770s were placed in charge of the Keepers who received payment from the Deputy Surveyor.

Exploitation of the Forest was common during the earlier part of the 18th century, though with the appointment of John Russell, Duke of Bedford, as Lord Warden of the New Forest in 1746 much of the corruption was dealt with and many officers, including Keepers, were turned out of their posts, often to be replaced by men of higher social standing and supposedly higher morals. The resulting improvement in the state of affairs brought about by the Duke of Bedford no doubt helped pave the way for the next incumbent of the post of Lord Warden, Prince William Henry, Duke of Gloucester and Edinburgh, who became Lord Warden in 1771.

In 1789, the Commissioners of Woods, Forests and Land Revenues published a report as to the state in which they found the Forest; among the evidence appended to the reports were interviews of all the Groom Keepers (previously known as Under Keepers) and a number of Master Keepers (previously known as Head or Chief Keepers) among other officers with roles on the Forest. By this stage it was clear that the office of the Master Keeper had become a sinecure – more a mark of patronage than a position of oversight and responsibility. The Groom Keepers again left to their own devices had strayed somewhat, many making money by alternative means. Two of them had managed to convert three of the newly planted inclosures into rabbit warrens, while one of the said Keepers was well respected for the breeding and training of gun dogs and had even trained a pig to point game, for which accomplishment she earned the rather undeserving name of 'Slut'. While the Groom Keepers had again become adept at exploiting their positions, the degree to which they did was on a much reduced scale.

The appointment of William Henry as Lord Warden was to see a period of 80 years during which the Crown's links with the Forest were at a high point. The Duke used his position to appoint a number of family members to officers on the Forest, with two of his children being appointed Master Keepers. Another Master Keeper was his nephew William Henry, son of George III, who was later to accede to the throne in 1830 as William IV. The Duke of Gloucester was succeeded as Lord Warden by another son of George III: Prince Frederick

Augustus, Duke of York and Albany. The latter appointed his brother, Prince Adolphus Frederick, Duke of Cambridge, as a Master Keeper, who became the last Lord Warden when appointed in 1845, at which time he appointed his son Prince George William Frederick Charles of Cambridge as a Master Keeper. When Adolphus died in 1850, the post of Lord Warden became defunct, along with the Master Keepers he appointed, while the Groom Keepers – thereafter known as Forest Keepers or just Keepers – were transferred to the Office of Woods, under the direction of the Deputy Surveyor.

A pressure which greatly increased during the 18th century and came to a head at the beginning of the 19th century was that of encroachments on the Forest. Many people had been driven from commons in southern England by the inclosure of the commons and this caused encroachment to peak in the mid-18th century. It was the Groom Keepers who were tasked with reporting the new encroachments to the Attachment and Swainmote Courts, at which forest law was administered, as well as throwing out inclosures by order of the Verderers. When in 1801 an enquiry into the encroachments was carried out, the Groom Keepers found themselves acting as key witnesses throughout the process. Later various statutes were passed to allow for the sale of the existing encroachments and purchase of small parcels of ground by adjacent landowners and so the rate of encroachments fell away, though the Keepers still have to deal with illegal encroachments today.

Another major change came to pass in the early 19th century with the appointment of Sylvester Douglas, Lord Glenbervie, as Surveyor General of Woods, Trent South. He was an energetic occupant of the post and spent much time looking to solve the problems he perceived as affecting the Forest. One of these was the *Divisium Imperium* and, as such, he was happy to increase the pay of the Keepers in exchange for a complete ban on creating new pollards. This increased his influence over a key office, while ending a perquisite that was seen as damaging to the interest of timber production. He was also the driving force behind an increase in the number of timber inclosures. These were made under an Act of Parliament of 1808 and set up on a more professional basis than those made previously. Each inclosure or group of inclosures was placed in the charge of a woodman who was provided with a cottage on site for his accommodation. The woodmen thereby relieved the Groom Keepers of their responsibility for protecting the inclosures.

In 1848, a Select Committee was appointed to report into the Crown's remaining forests, with the New Forest attracting attention early on. The state of affairs there was found to have gone so far awry that three reports (as opposed to one) were needed to complete the inquiry. Major concerns centred around the actions of an assistant to the Assistant Deputy Surveyor who was exploiting timber on the Forest, a course of action he was able to follow due to the lack of oversight from the Deputy Surveyor

Left: Keeper Jack Humby, Mr Babey, Keeper Harry Blandford, Keeper Albert Humby, Mr Wren, (old) Bert Smith, Arthur Duell (Langley Wood Estate employee who probably transported the deer with a horse and cart), Alf (Gaffer) Green (Langley Wood Head Forester and Uncle to New Forest Keepers Jack and Albert Humby), Head Keeper George Blake, Jack Bridge (Langley Wood Estate employee). Front with stag Monty Slightam. 1936.
Right: Rabbit clearance on Long Slade Bottom near Brockenhurst. Four men set out on a patrol through the Forest, where they shot rabbits that fed during the evening on newly planted trees, 1957. Willy Gulliver, Keeper at Burley, Monty Slightam, Keeper at Wilverley, Frank Breakspear, Head Keeper and driving was Wilf Cook Keeper at Aldridge Hill.

who had largely abandoned his post due to 'ill health'. Though the Groom Keepers were not to come away unscathed and two were dismissed for illegally taking wood from their Walks.

The 1848 Select Committee report was a key driver for major changes to the management of the New Forest that led to the 1851 Deer Removal Act, which not only spelt doom for the Forest's deer but also led to further large-scale inclosure of the Forest landscape and the first large-scale planting of conifers. The following three years saw an almost total eradication of the deer, with the Groom Keepers largely responsible for reducing the numbers. With the deer gone, the need for a large staff of Keepers was deemed unnecessary and their numbers were slashed to six, some of their lodges were leased out to wealthy gentry and their Walks combined.

The 1850s also saw the review of common rights and the enforcement of certain medieval restrictions as to the turn out of commonable stock. In the early 1860s, the Verderers ordered the Groom Keepers to undertake a drift of stock to enforce the restrictions, but they refused to take orders from Verderers. Thereafter the Keepers were no longer involved in stock management and the Agisters took over the role.

In 1880, Gerald Lascelles was appointed Deputy Surveyor and he soon found that the reduction in the number of Keepers and appointment of labourers as Under Keepers had led to a very unsatisfactory state of affairs. Many had a sideline in the sale of rare birds, taking Kingfishers and birds of prey to supply local taxidermists. Lascelles, who took a great deal of interest in wildlife and in particular birds, took a dim view of this and took steps to end the trade and place the Keepers on a footing to preserve wildlife. As a first step he managed to acquire a fifth Head Keeper (their numbers had been allowed to dwindle to just four) and he swept away the Forest's ancient system of Bailiwicks and Walks, so that each Head Keeper took charge of one of five Districts, while the 12 Under Keeper were placed *en masse* under them rather than acting independently as had previously been the case. All Keepers were issued with printed orders and rules, which also detailed their duties. They were also sworn in as special constables to combat incendiary fires that were being directed against the new inclosures, which the Commoners saw as encroaching on their rights. To appease the Commoners the burning of heathland was introduced, in 1881, to improve grazing. Previously, burning was restricted to strips alongside the railway and around the new inclosures as fire breaks.

Lascelles can be considered the father of the present day Keeper's team. He wrote:

> *"A strong staff of Keepers... is a necessity in the New Forest, apart altogether from any questions of preservation of game or of sport. They are the custodians who do all the policing of the public property, and their duties are manifold."*

Lascelles continued in post until 1914 and ten years later the wooded Crown Estates were transferred, under the Transfer of Woods Act 1923, to the newly formed Forestry Commission. This was to be the start of a new era, though the changes made by Lascelles were to stand the Keepers in good stead.

With the coming of the Forestry Commission the Forest was placed on a different footing – an altogether more commercial one. A much greater emphasis was placed on the planting of conifers over broad-leaved trees, thus changing the nature of the Forest considerably.

Old aspects of the Keepers' workload gradually died out, such as shooting the bounds, whereby the Keepers would enter the private lands on the Forest and discharge their guns to maintain the right of the Crown to sport over those estates; though since the 19th century landowners were allowed to buy out these rights. The collection of Forest dues which were largely related to the exercise of common rights were similarly sold out and those which remained were abandoned in the 1960s as their fixed nature meant they were no longer worth the trouble collecting.

However, something that did return were the deer and it didn't take that long after the Deer Removal Act for the number to increase again, but the two World Wars certainly helped and the Keepers once again saw deer management become a central part of their jobs.

During the World Wars, the Keepers found themselves in reserved occupations but still very much involved in the war effort as the Forest was used for the concentration and training of troops, particularly during the Second World War. During the latter they were absorbed into special auxiliary units set up to remain behind lines in the event of an invasion. Less secret was their involvement on the Hampshire War Agricultural Committee, where their knowledge of the Forest was useful in identifying those areas of the Forest where the grazing could be improved or areas set aside for agricultural production. The Keepers work was also increased by an expansion of the controlled burning programme to meet the increased threat of wildfires caused by allied training and enemy action alike.

The mechanisation which was brought to the fore during the war years soon found itself impacting on the Forest with large-scale drainage impacting sites across the Forest. With the burning regime maintained at high levels, the Forest continued to be seen as an area for production both agriculturally and silviculturally, with the heavy wartime felling followed by further coniferization. The result caused great damage to the wildlife interest of the Forest, and a newly introduced alien – the Grey Squirrel – came to thrive, thereby adding to the Keepers' workload due to their bark stripping tendencies. While responsible for some of the work, the Keepers also represented the wildlife interest, a role which was to be encouraged by a new Deputy Surveyor, Arthur Cadman, who was appointed to the post in

NEW FOREST KEEPERS 1953.

G. W. E. Smith   W. Gulliver

H. W. Blandford   J. M. Slightam   J. Humby   B. Bessant   R. J. Cutler   W. A. Humby   A. P. Breakspear   G. A. J. Barrel

B. B. Smith   F. E. B. de Uphaugh   E. Wynne Jones   H. F. Young   W. G. Blake.

1959. Very much a sportsman naturalist he dedicated his book *Dawn, Dusk and Deer*, published in 1966, 'To the Keepers of the New Forest who have taught me so much.' It was in 1959 that an agreement was drawn up between the Nature Conservancy (now Natural England) and the Forestry Commission to consult over the management of the Forest, which was therein recognised as being of National Nature Reserve status and certain areas were designated primarily as nature reserves. It was not, however, purely a period of increased protection, for a protracted battle was fought against the Forestry Commission during the 1960s to prevent the commercial exploitation of the Open Forest woodlands which had been given special protection as far back as 1877. The battle led to the signing of the Minister's Mandate in 1971, which clarified issues relating to the management of the Forest, while the same year the entire Forest was designated a Site of Special Scientific Interest. Other local, national and international wildlife designations have followed, confirming the importance of the Keepers in their role as wildlife managers.

Another major post-war change has been the increase in visitor numbers, with the car bringing increasingly more people to the Forest. The Keepers got their first vehicles in around 1950 but it would be a while before they all had one. Dealing with bye-law enforcement became a major part of their work, though the use of the Verderers' Court to prosecute offenders fell out of use in the 1960s. The 1970s saw recreation controlled through the provision of camping sites and car parks, which added to the work of the Keepers though they no longer had campers queuing outside their cottages on summer weekends to get a camping permit. Not until the 1990s were Recreation Rangers introduced. Until that time the whole weight of the work fell onto the shoulders of the Keepers, while the use of the Forest has continued at a pace that outstrips any recent additions made to staffing.

In more recent time economic factors have led to a reduction in staffing in an attempt to balance the books, this at a time when more and more pressure is mounting on the Forest and more and more is being asked of the Keepers. This seems a retrograde step: no doubt Deputy Surveyor Lascelles would have considered that a 'strong staff of keepers' is needed more than ever.

New Forest Buckhounds

W as it King Canute or William the Conqueror who names the New Forest 'Ytene? (A Royal Hunting Forest).

It is well documented that William the Conqueror was passionate about the deer for hunting and thus their preservation.

1815 saw the passing of The Deer Removal Act. Two years of slaughter only sought the deer to leave the Forest and seek refuge in adjoining land holdings. It is a similar situation today.

In 1883 the Deputy Surveyor, The Honourable Gerald Lacelles, put hunting on a formal footing. Mr. Buckworth Powell had a few couple of hounds. It was Mr. Francis Lovell of Hincheslea kennelled hounds and hunted from August to April excluding October (the rutting season).

So The New Forest Deerhounds (Buckhounds) started to hunt the Forest properly two days a week. Both red and fallow male deer being hunted.

It was very much part of the New Forest Keepers' duty to harbour a warrantable deer for the hounds.

The hound is a very unique complex animal. Time and time again when the tufters (hounds used to rouse and single out a deer from the gang) were laid on to a gang of male deer, it was often the hounds settled on to the scent of the appropriate animal. The hounds' instinct knowing which one to hunt. In much the same way the wolf or the lynx would choose their quarry. (There is talk about re-introducing them to help control deer numbers!)

Perhaps we should be more understanding – man

should be made to suit the deer and not the deer made to suit man.

The Buckhounds continued their role as the True Guardians of the Deer, until 1997 when the decision was made to disband. The deer lost the Best Friend they had – the hound.

Many social events were arranged across the Forest. Holding the Forest community, supporters and friends together. The Buckhounds dances were particularly well supported – the well known band Peter Pod and The Peas were a huge attraction.
Ye Olde Fallowe Bucke

Brock Mair, Kennel Huntsman of the New Forest Buckhounds, at the Opening Meet at Long Cross Pond, 1926.

Keepers Profiles

A rare photograph of all the New Forest Keepers together, which I took during the shoot for their page in the book *Keepers*. Left to right: Andy Shore, Alan Stride, Patrick Cook, Maarten Ledeboer, Matthew Davies, Howard Taylor, Andy Page, Graham Wilson, Jonathan Cook, Ian Young, Tim Creed.

Historically, the head of the Forestry Commission in the New Forest has always carried the title of Deputy Surveyor and this is still the case today. There is no role of 'Surveyor' that currently exists or has existed over the past few centuries. The Forestry Commission manages the Forest on behalf of the Crown.

Bruce Rothnie

"Our most inspiring landscapes have often developed from a long association with man. Ever since man has chosen to settle and farm, he has learnt to observe his local surroundings, understand the seasonal patterns of its nature and sought to work in harmony with its natural pace.

The New Forest is one of the finest examples of landscapes in the UK today that is the outcome of a long and rich heritage of interaction with man.

Despite the pressures of modern society its management remains surprisingly attuned to the ways established by those early observers.

But as modern man gets ever more efficient in finding and exploiting the resources society needs for its survival, the number of people with our forefathers' inherent understanding of their surroundings is diminishing. Despite the massive growth in information and understanding in the scientific world we ignore the intrinsic knowledge of the people who live and work in the landscape every day at our peril. Their knowledge and wisdom regulates our temptations for rapid change and quick gratification.

The Forestry Commission is the current custodian of the Crown Lands of the New Forest. It is charged with managing these lands on behalf of the nation to sustain their special qualities and to work in

close partnership with the commoning community.

I have seen at first hand the immense value that Forestry Commission staff, many of whom have worked unbroken in the New Forest for decades, add in shaping the land and the wildlife that thrive upon it. No staff group epitomises this more strongly than the New Forest Keepers.

For these men (and now women too!) their role is not a job but a calling. All hold a strong regard for the heritage of the post of New Forest Keeper and a deep commitment for their role as guardians of the Forest. All have an innate passion to put the protection of the Forest first. Each lives within their 'beat' on the Forest and knows it more intimately than anyone else. Their insight comes from a relentless energy to learn from their place through observation and experience accrued over many years. Not only observing the wildlife, but observing a remarkably diverse range of human behaviour too!

Most people will not appreciate how much the work of the Keepers is helping to enhance the Forest for the future. We all benefit from their dedication. This book provides a small insight into the extent of their devotion to duty."

Andy Page
Head Keeper and Head of Wildlife Management, Andy has been part of the team for 29 years.

He started his working career in 1974 as a gamekeeper on a private estate adjacent to the New Forest, and after 13 years applied for the post of New Forest Keeper with the intention of acquiring experience in deer management and, more importantly, nature conservation.

He was promoted to Head Keeper after ten years, with responsibility for the northern half of the Forest. When the Head Keeper for the South of the Forest retired in 2010, Andy became responsible for the whole Keeper team. In addition, he was then appointed Head of Wildlife Management for the wider South England District of Dorset and Sussex with an additional six Wildlife Rangers.

He wrote the current South District Deer Management plan, which aims to maintain the tradition and heritage of the fallow deer, from its origins over a thousand years ago as the beast of the chase for the king, to its place in a modern multi-use Forest.

'I also oversee the annual cut-and-burn programme for the management of the Forest's heathland, while taking into consideration the rare and threatened species that make it their home,' he explains. 'I can deliver conservation advice to the Forester team to enable timber harvesting to continue with minimal impact on our wildlife.'

Andy's life-long passion has been studying the bird life of the Forest and he has written numerous articles and given talks on the subject. He has been involved in monitoring and recording the scarcer birds of prey by ringing and data recording and also through the use of nest cams. This has helped protect breeding sites from Forestry activities while amassing useful population data for both local and national ornithological bodies. More recently he has taken a keen interest in Lepidoptera, particularly moths.

He regards himself as extremely lucky to have met and worked with so many passionate and knowledgeable people from numerous conservation, environmental and sporting organisations, who are working to protect this unique place from the many challenges the modern world is throwing at it. He regards himself as having had the privilege of helping to shape and mould the Forest through a time of significant change, with enlightened Forest design plans and groundbreaking river and wetland restoration projects. These measures leave him hugely optimistic that the Forest will continue far into the future and remain a very special place for wildlife.

Jonathan Cook
Jonathan Cook went to Sparsholt College and started work as a Forestry Commission Ranger in what was then the West Downs Forest District in May 1979. He progressed quickly, and when New Forest Keeper Harold Cutler retired, Jonathan applied for the job. He was offered the position and moved into Stockley Cottage in August 1989.

His responsibility has been managing the sika herd, which are largely confined to his beat within the Crown lands. He is also passionate about protecting the Forest and all its wildlife and culture. He is robust but fair in dealing with those who would choose to abuse the New Forest and has many letters of commendation for his diligence and fairness in dealing with a multitude of incidents involving the public, be it missing persons, injured riders, lost dogs, or cases of pollution and poaching.

He has also played a major part in the reintroduction of the pearl-bordered fritillary butterfly.

Patrick Cook
Patrick has been a New Forest Keeper for 11 years. 'I joined the Forestry Commission in 1989 and took up the role of Wildlife Ranger managing wild deer populations in the South Midlands. After 15 years a wonderful opportunity arose to take up a position in the historic New Forest as a Keeper. I jumped at the chance. The prospect of working in the former Royal hunting forest with its history and associated traditions was very appealing. I thoroughly enjoy the role and in particular the diversity of work it provides. No day at work is ever the same. I also enjoy the chance to apply my knowledge and help shape the Forest for the future.'

Tim Creed
Retired to France in 2015 after 26 years service as a New Forest Keeper.

On leaving the army in 1986, Tim Creed joined the Forestry Commission as a Wildlife Ranger on the Marches in Shropshire. One of his jobs was to manage the long haired fallow of the Mortimer Forest. These were discovered and documented in 1953 by Gerald Springthorpe, the Head Wildlife Ranger, and titled *Dama dama springthorpeii* after him. They do not occur anywhere else in the world.

Tim was also involved with the bat box scheme and brought those skills to the New Forest where he transferred as a Keeper with his own beat in 1989. In addition to doing the job that he loved, he enjoyed being part of the Forest community and as a Commoner he ran ponies and pigs on the Forest and he kept bees.

He appreciated and misses all the wildlife and the flora and fauna. He followed all three hunts on foot – the Buckhounds, the New Forest Hounds and the Beagles. Overall he delighted in the magic of the New Forest and valued the opportunity of working there.

Matthew Davies
Matthew has been a Keeper for 27 years but says it seems more like a couple of years.

'I joined the Forestry Commission on 4th September 1989. I had left Sparsholt college in the summer and needed a job. Gamekeepers change employment in February so I took this position to wait for something suitable to come up, but I have yet to find anything comparable!'

Maarten Lebeboer
Originally from the Netherlands, Maarten has been a Keeper since 2002.

'From a young age I have been interested in the outdoors, especially in forests and their wildlife. After studying at the International Agricultural College Larenstein, in the Netherlands, and completing my Forestry and Wildlife degree study, I was looking to gain some experience overseas. I came over to the New Forest to start work experience with the Forestry Commission in 1999, and never went home again! I worked briefly for the Forestry and Harvesting department before I became the first "foreign" New Forest Keeper.'

'The main reason why I love the New Forest Keeper role so much is the opportunity to work "hands-on" in one of the most important Ancient Forests of Europe. To protect it and look after it is a real privilege but also safeguards its future. It's a lovely and unique place to work. Together with my wife and little daughter, we really value its beauty and tranquillity on a daily basis as we live in a Keepers cottage in the middle of the Forest on a busy beat.

'The role of a New Forest Keeper is very varied and as I get involved with a wide range of land management issues I never get bored – each day and night is different. Although I like all aspects of my role, I especially enjoy the deer management. The New Forest deer herds are a major historic component of the landscape; they need to be managed with respect. My other interests are wild boar and butterflies; my beat contains some rare fritillary species, which need delicate management.'

Andy Shore
Andy has worked for the Forestry Commission for 28 years and has been a Keeper in the New Forest for 23 of them

'I was brought up on a smallholding on the New Forest and we lived on whatever we reared, grew, caught or shot. I started cover beating on Broadlands Estate aged ten under Head Keeper Harry Grass and Underkeepers Bill Webb and Tony Paine. Keeping was all I was ever going to do.

'I worked on a local estate for a couple of years, before joining the Forestry Commission. I was one of a few that were lucky enough to work with the very last of the "Old School" Keepers, many of who were taken on as boys by my great-uncle, Head Keeper Bert Smith.

'Uncle Bert was not a man that embraced modern ways of thought or action. I once asked him what had had the most impact on the Forest in his lifetime. He said, when the Forestry Commission took over from the Crown Office of Woods in 1924 and the massive impact of the tarmac lorries that metalled the Forest tracts, which brought so many people, and dogs, here – something it would never recover from, in his eyes.

'In 1932, I think, grey squirrels were released at Emery Down. They were protected for five years, until it was realised that they carried a disorder which ultimately helped destroy the reds, and from that point the Keepers were instructed to trap or shoot every one. Needless to say they didn't succeed and the battle still goes on. Greys have had an extremely negative impact on our Forest trees and vulnerable small wildlife.

'It couldn't be more of an honour to be a Crown Keeper. Whatever the negative parts of our work, they are more than outweighed by being able to care for the Forest and bring up our families in such a special and unique place. My love of wildlife and the Forest has never dimmed.'

Sandy Shore

Sandy has worked for the Forestry Commission for 11 years and became a New Forest Keeper in 2015. There have always been strong family connections with the New Forest and her grandfather started work for the Forestry Commission in 1952. She was born in Aldershot because her father was in the Royal Logistic Corps, but he returned to the Forest when she was three years old because her parents wanted to bring up their children in the New Forest.

She has always felt very strongly about working in the New Forest and her work experience with the Keeper team, while she was still at college, confirmed to her where she wanted to be. She is a licensed bat handler and has also recently completed a course on handling dangerous reptiles and amphibians. She is the first female Keeper and is married to Keeper Andy Shore. They have two small children who they are bringing up in the commoning tradition.

Alan Stride

Alan has been part of the New Forest Keepers team for four years.

'I was born in Lyndhurst in the New Forest, and brought up in Brook where my family have lived for five generations,' he says. As a boy he worked with his father, Raymond Stride, who was the Keeper and estate worker at Warrens in Bramshaw. They used to help on other estates and he followed the New Forest Hounds and the Buckhounds. He continued at Warrens when he left school, and then joined Forestry Commission contractor Jeff Kitcher in his timber business before moving over to the Forestry Commission, where he spent 18 years felling timber.

When he applied for the job as a Keeper he spent 18 months working under the then Head Keeper John Gulliver and the South Walk team and in 2012 he moved into his cottage as a New Forest Keeper.

'I particularly enjoy wildlife conservation and managing habitat clearance for butterflies with volunteers,' he says, and is very proud of the fact that along with Jonathan Cook's beat they have the best pearl-bordered fritillaries in the south of England. He's had a shotgun and firearms licence since the age of 17, and part of his job involves controlling the vermin and helping with the annual deer cull.

Howard Taylor

This is Howard's 25th year as a New Forest Keeper.

'The New Forest has always been a fascination of mine. During my schooldays my father and I would make annual fishing trips to Hampshire, fishing the River Avon to the Forest's west and the River Test to the east. We would stay within the bounds of the New Forest at a B&B run by a retired river keeper and his wife, where on late summer evenings he would tell me tales of forests and rivers. I listened for hours: the spawning sea trout within the Forest streams, the large deer herds and above all the New Forest Keepers.

'From an early age I aspired to be a New Forest Keeper, to work beneath the ancient trees,

manage the deer, and put something back into this magnificent Forest, but it would be later in my career when I would find myself with this wonderful opportunity. From working as a gamekeeper in Kent and Surrey I slowly worked my way westward, where for a while I worked as a river keeper on the beautiful River Dever before studying biology at university in my 20s. Every six months or so I would write to the Forestry Commission and enquire about vacancies for Forest Keepers. One day I received a brown envelope containing a job description and an application form. I completed it, sat the interview and was offered the job – I thought I must be dreaming!'

Graham Wilson

With 52 years in the New Forest, Graham is its longest serving Keeper. He also has a responsibility to the Forest Estates.

Graham Wilson's immense knowledge and wide circle of contacts are legendary.

His father was a friend of the Head Keeper Jack Humby. So when the young Graham left school his father asked if there were any jobs going at the Forestry Commission. Graham had been doing holiday jobs with Jack Humby so he applied for the position of trainee Keeper in July 1964 and succeeded. He doesn't hesitate to acknowledge how incredibly fortunate he was and admits that much of what he knows he learned from Jack Humby. He witnessed his people skills: 'Mr Humby treated everyone the same, whether they were a gypsy or Lord Montagu,' he says.

During this three-year training he lived in a caravan at Bull Hill and cycled over to Mr Humby at Stockley Cottage. Once, he was on his way there when he noticed a parked Morris 1100. When he approached he saw the driver was slumped over and looking further he realised he was dead. Shocked, the boy pedalled furiously over to Mr Humby who insisted on finishing his breakfast before going to look. After all the man 'wasn't going anywhere'. He had cut his throat. That was the first of many suicides Graham has had to deal with as a Keeper.

After three years he was promoted to probationary Keeper and the Forestry Commission created a small beat for him so he was on his own but watched over by some of the greatest Keepers the Forest has ever known. They included Jack and his brother Albert Humby, Harry Blandford, Willie Gulliver, Gerald Barrell, Harold Cutler and John Frankcom. When Albert Humby retired Graham took his Keeper position at Kings Hat in 1969 and covered the whole of the South East fringe. He says that he can't overemphasise how good Jack Humby was to him and how privileged he was to have worked with such a man.

Today, he probably works seven days a week, and as a Commoner runs cattle and ponies on the Forest. He has followed all the Forest hunts and loves all the hounds. He says that the job is a vocation.

Ian Young

He has been a Keeper since 1987. He retired in 2012 and now works as a volunteer.

Ian has never left the Forest except when he went to see the Rolling Stones at Twickenham in 2006 and the O2 in 2012. He worked seven days a week and since retirement has been a volunteer

Keeper because he so loves the job. He works closely with Keeper Andy Shore on the controlled burning programme because they have always worked well together. They can spend the whole day together and never speak because they both know what the other is doing.

Born in Furzey Lodge in 1946 among the Gullivers (a long line of Keepers) and the commoning Kitchers, he joined the Forestry Commission in 1962 as a Warrener. He was tasked to catch rabbits in and around freshly planted trees to prevent damage, as well as to catch squirrels in the spring when they are notorious for stripping the bark off trees, especially the beech trees. He then became a trainee Keeper and was appointed a Keeper in 1987 and moved into Aldridge Hill Cottage.

In addition to commoning he made it his business to go to Parish Council meetings and the Verderers' Court because he thought it important to be in constant contact with the public.

'Before 1970 campers could pitch their tents anywhere except within 100 yards of the inclosures because of fire risk. They bought their licence from the local Keeper's cottage. Now they have to pitch their tent on campsites,' he says.

There is no doubt in his mind that his most important job was managing the red deer and he still loves them. He used to manage 120, but the herd has now been culled down to a healthy 80. Although an indigenous breed, the Deer Removal Act of 1851 meant that officially there were no red deer on the Forest. However it is rumoured that in 1962/3 red deer from private herds, such as Sir Dudley Forwood's at Burley Old House, escaped on to the Forest due to fallen trees on fence lines. They made their way over from Burley Rocks to Ober Heath via Markway.

In 1908 the Beaulieu Estate introduced one red deer stag and two hinds on Hartford Heath. They ran on the south of the Forest between Brockenhurst Manor and Exbury Estate.

Ian worked closely with the local landowners to make sure that the red stags were not shot when they wandered on to private land. With the help of the British Deer Society and volunteers, he had four deer lawns created on his beat especially for the red deer.

Ian believes all New Forest Keepers should be Commoners because everyone has to work together on the Forest. If a Commoner or Agister sees an illegal camper he tells the Keeper and if a Keeper sees a distressed or injured pony he tells the Agister.

New Forest National Park

This beautiful book will undoubtedly help in the important task of explaining how the New Forest works. It is an extraordinary part of England, and is arguably the most heavily protected landscape in the country, and also its smallest and most besieged National Park.

Yet it has survived largely untouched for almost 1,000 years since it was created by William the Conqueror as one of his many new royal hunting forests. As such it is blessed with ancient traditions and institutions, of which the Keepers are one. Their main role as managers of the wildlife perfectly complements that of the Forest's other venerable institution, the Verderers' Court.

The work of the Keepers is discreet, almost secret, and requires a deep understanding of all the Forest's wild creatures and its matchless landscape, from salmon to sika, from burning gorse to cutting bracken. The Keepers also need to control the many recreational activities that now take place on the open Forest, which are diverse and range from mass orienteering events to flying model aeroplanes. It is a busy place, but as remote as ever once you stray off the beaten track, and effectively enter the Keepers' true kingdom.

As a newly created organisation, and the New Forest's youngest, the National Park Authority is ultimately responsible for ensuring that the landscape is protected on behalf of the nation, and that the general public understand and respect it.

Above: Red deer in winter.
Opposite: Sika in the woods.

Without the work of the Keepers that task would not
be possible, and this book helps explain why.
Oliver Crosthwaite-Eyre DL Chairman of the New
Forest National Park Authority

Afterword
Sally Fear

The idea for this book came in 2010 when I read an impassioned letter in *The Lymington Times*, from 'the son of a New Forest Keeper and the grandson of a Head Keeper' – John Cutler. John's letter was written in response to an item in that same newspaper which was by Anthony Pasmore, a Verderer of the New Forest. At the time it looked as if the jobs of the New Forest Keepers were in jeopardy. The government was considering cutting their team from 12 to 6, and it seemed it was just because nobody really understood what they do. The great fear was that the New Forest stood to lose nearly a thousand years of experience gained through the continuity of a dedicated New Forest Keeper team. This would undoubtedly have harmed our national heritage.

I am pleased to say that the government changed its mind and the Keepers of the New Forest remain in their job. We now have ten, though one is also Head of Wildlife and one is also responsible for the Estates.

I am a Commoner of the New Forest and I have published two books on the Commoning way of life, but I knew little about the Forest's Keepers. I asked my Keeper friend Tim Creed if he thought the Keepers would like me to produce a book on their work in a similar way to my approach to the Commoners. He spoke with his colleagues and the response was wholeheartedly positive. Of course neither the Keepers nor myself realised what we had taken on. So I have spent much time deep in the heart of New Forest recording the work of the modern day New Forest Keepers (when I can find them!) and the great

variety of wildlife, flora and fauna that they manage.

All too often we find ourselves caught up in the distractions of daily life. The work of the Keepers allows us to pause and take a moment to find the focus to navigate through what comes next. Their wealth of knowledge and ancient culture fits well into a modern world. It is a way of life that is ordered by the seasons and the work that they demand. It has been that way for hundreds of years.

These modern photographs of an ancient landscape show a deep-rooted attachment to place. They portray a way of life that is little noticed by most and yet has profoundly shaped history, and will continue to do so.

The New Forest Keepers' year offers a unique account of rural life and a fundamental connection with the land that most of us have lost. It is a story of working lives, a people who exist and endure even as the world changes around them. It is authentic. It is the real thing.

He made large forests for the deer and enacted laws therewith, so that whoever killed a hart or a hind should be killed.

Anglo Saxon Chronicle 1087 referring to William The Conqueror

I would like to thank His Royal Highness The Duke of Edinburgh for his thoughtful and generous Foreword.

Robin Page for his Introduction combined with his interest and kindness.

My husband Richard Harris-Jones for his encouragement and constant support.

Stuart Smith, Claudia Paladini, Justine Schuster and Rob Hucker at SMITH-Design.

Thank you to the following Authors for their inspiring and informative specialist writing: Alison Bolton for the Wildflowers, Sara Cadbury for the Fungi, Andy Page for the Birds, Richard Reeves for the History, John Ruppersbery for the Butterflies and the The Reverend Nicky Davies.

Bruth Rothnie, Dominic May and Oliver Crosthwaite-Eyre, and for their Forest text.

The Forestry Commission for the use of their Keepers' beat map.

Willy and Gwen Gulliver, Graham Wilson and Susan Niccolls for the use of their historical photographs. Tony Johnson and Robin Street for their historical support. I apologise for not crediting or thanking any contributor that I could not contact.

Thank you to the estates of Pablo Neruda, Colin Tubbs, Ray Bradbury, Arthur Cadman, Albert Camus, George Herbert for the use of their quotes.

A book of this kind is inevitably a collaborative venture, and during the photography and production I have incurred a great many debts of gratitude for help, advice and guidance. The first debt is of course to the Crown Keepers of the New Forest and their families for giving their time, patience, support and enthusiasm. To them I extend my heartfelt appreciation. Without them this book would not have happened. Also the many other people who have supported me throughout, in no particular order and apologies to those I have not mentioned: Lynne Patchett MVO, Brigadier Archie Miller-Bakewell, Rosamond Castle, Jayne Albery FC, Denise Eccles FC, Verderer Barry Dowsett, Ian and Tracy Thew, Dorothy Ireland of the British Deer Society, John Fawcett, Paula Blakeby, Amanda Mann, Will Day, Kristen Harrison, photographers: Christopher Cormack, David Reed, Philippe Achache, Patrick Ward, Christopher Angeloglou, Matt Stuart.

My medical team – traditional and alternative – who have managed my back throughout: John Nixon Orthopaedic Surgeon, Robert Lever Cranial Osteopath, Cathy Rowlandson Physiotherapist and Marion Watt Bowens Therapist who came to save me several times during unsocial hours when I couldn't move.

Page 2: A fallow fawn in the long grass.
Page 4: New Forest Keeper Ian Young walking through the woods with his beagles after rabbit shooting.
Page 6: A red stag.
Pages 8-9: A red stag approaches a hind.

HRH The Duke of Edinburgh is a Patron of the Wildscreen Charity, whose 'goal is to convene the best photographers, filmmakers and creative professionals with the most committed conservationists to create compelling stories about the natural world; that inspire the wider public to experience it, feel part of it and protect it.'

Robin Page is a naturalist, author and Telegraph columnist. He is Founder and Chairman of the Countryside Restoration Trust, which is a 'farming and wildlife charity – demonstrating how to produce quality food commercially, but in a wildlife friendly way'.

A percentage of the profits from the sales of this book will be given to both these Charities.

First published in an edition of
2000 copiesin 2016 by Tile Barn Farm
sallyfear.com

© Sally Fear
Images © Sally Fear
Text © Sally Fear
and various authors

Design by SMITH
Robert Hucker, Claudia Paladini, Justine Schuster

Printed in Italy by EBS

British Library cataloguing-in-publication data.
A catalogue record of this book is available from the British Library.

ISBN 978-0-9562643-1-2